Two Bites of the Cherry

Two Bites of the Cherry

by

Sidney Talbot

The Pentland Press Limited
Edinburgh · Cambridge · Durham

First published in 1993 by
The Pentland Press Ltd.
1 Hutton Close
South Church
Bishop Auckland
Durham

ISBN 1 85821 133 6

Typeset by Elite Typesetting Techniques, Southampton.
Printed and bound by Antony Rowe Ltd., Chippenham.

Acknowledgements

Gratitude is expressed to Alan Bloom for his valuable advice and to Mrs Lanstaf, Mrs Easto and Mrs Clutten for the use of photographs.

Thanks are also due to my daughter-in-law, Jacqueline, for her help in deciphering these memories from my original handwritten script and to Lizzie Hammond for typing the text ready for presentation to the publishers.

Last of all, gratitude to my wife, Nora, for her endless help and tolerance.

> I dedicate this book to my son,
> Raymond, and to the memory of my
> late son, Russell, who both
> inspired me to write this recording
> of my life.

Preface

When I was first asked to write a book on my memories, I decided to write one quite different from the usual run of books on that subject. Such as stating facts all the time, as no one needs a history lesson every time they read one's life story.

This book is about how I saw life as it came to meet me and how I responded to all its challenges. Everyone whose life has spanned three quarters of a century as mine has have had a wonderful chance to look back on the many and varied changes as no other era will experience.

We have seen the change from steam to diesel and then to electricity for the driving force of ships and trains. We also remember the clanging of the trams and the coming of the motor car. Candles in my boyhood days were interchanged with oil lamps and then taken over by electricity and gas. Silent pictures were taken over by the talkies, the television took over our houses. Men have landed on the moon. Women press a few buttons for the week's wash.

All these things and a lot more we, in our age group, have seen happen in the space of a lifetime.

Sidney Talbot
July 1992

Contents

Chapter 1

First Impressions – Stone Picking

'What lovely shuttles your boy has got Libby!' They were the very first words I can remember from way back in the First World War days. The year was 1916 and I was just three years old. The occasion was when my mother (Libby) and several other women of our small parish of Thelveton were busy trying to earn a few extra shillings by flintstone picking. The fields seemed to be full of them in those days. The person who had said those words to my mother was a lady by the name of Bella, who came from the next village. She was a well-known lady, quaint but shrewd, as I was soon to find out. Mother used to take me with her stone picking and in the pram was some home-brewed beer, which my father, in common with other men of those days, used to brew each year. Bella was there to look after me while Mother worked. Every now and again Mother would come to the pram at the end of the field for a little refreshment. On the occasion when Bella spoke of my eyes (or shuttles as they were sometimes called) Mother noticed Bella was a bit unsteady on her feet and said 'You have been at my beer again. I asked you to look after Sidney, I think I had better take the rest of this beer down the field with me or you will get drunk!' I can remember those words very clearly, at the same time I began to think 'Why are they picking stones at all?' Even in those very early days I used to ask 'Why?' and that has remained with me all my life whenever anything happens I think 'why?' The answer to my thoughts about the stone picking soon became obvious and as time went by the whole sequence unfolded before my very young eyes.

Flintstones were always needed to make roadways up on the farm and, as I was to find out, for the county's roads too, as when I was walking with Mother we came across this heap of stones on the side of the road with a man sitting there with a pair of metal goggles on, wielding a hammer,

1

The Stone Breaker 1916.

breaking up the biggest stones to a uniform size. I have often thought since; what a way to spend your working life, earning perhaps 13/– a week. Women picked them in the first place and what a job that was! The farmers would put a tumbril in the field where stones were to be picked, the women would have pails to collect the stones and they would tip these, when filled, into the tumbril. To fill the tumbril would take several hours - perhaps all day and the farmer would collect it later. At the end of the week the women would be paid 1/– each per tumbril load. Sometimes there would be four women, sometimes only two; in other words the more women who went, the easier it was, but some women in those days were very jealous of each other earning extra money and would rather work

The Author aged 1 year.

harder for their money than 'old Mrs So and So' given the chance. I heard all these things and wondered 'why?' Since the farmer paid 5/– for the whole load, I often wondered who came off best! The extra money was very welcome as the pay in those days was very low for a farm worker – 13/– a week.

When the stones were collected they were taken to the side of the road which was about to be repaired and left until required, which might be in a year's time.

Others would be deposited in the farmyards and stackyards for the farmer's own use. Some would be used for land drainage: yes, there were many uses for stones.

Chapter 2

I Start School

Hearing my parents talk, and from what I gleaned from others, I realized there was a lot going on around me I ought to know about. At that very early age – I was four years old – my thirst for other things began to show. I felt different and wanted to be with the other children, several of whom had visited our house with their mothers at one time or another (mostly girls), all older than me, and I would watch them going to school every day, which was only 200 yards down the road. So one day, without my mother's knowledge, I waited by the gate at dinner time for the big girls to go back to school, then ran out onto the road, grabbed one of the girls by the hand, and said 'Take me to school with you'. Ann, whose hand I was clutching, said 'Will your mother mind?' I said 'No'. When we got to school, the teacher said 'You can stay; I will put you in Miss Cook's class,' (she was the infant teacher). 'In the meantime I will send someone to find out if you should be here.' I liked what I had seen so far and was hopeful that Mother would let me stay, which, fortunately, she did, after a lot of talking about my age – four years and four months. The school I attended all my school days was very small; the greatest number of pupils I remember attending was 28 but the average was 23. There were two teachers: Miss Grace Cook was the infant teacher; she came each day from Dickleburgh where her father was a pork butcher. Miss Cook was a great favourite with everyone, showing plenty of patience and kindness to all her pupils. Mrs Munslow was the Head Teacher and she had two daughters and a son. I did not know much about her teaching, as by the time I reached the top class she had left and been replaced. The teacher who followed her was a good teacher but very strict. Many a pupil felt the sting of her cane when the need arose!

5

The Author aged 4 years.

Having given a taste of conditions and the very early days of my life, I feel that at this stage I should enlighten the reader regarding the life of a country boy and the village he lived in from that very early day in 1916 when this story began.

I was born in the village of Rushall, then moved to Bungay where, I understand, we lived at Shadow Barn. This was at the time of the 'Murder at the Red Barn', so I heard my parents say. When I was two years old we moved to Thelveton, where this story begins.

The village of Thelveton was owned by and under the control of Sir Edward Mann Bt. who lived in The Hall with his family. He was known as 'The Squire' and was very strict but at the same time was kind to everyone. His wife, Lady Mann, was also strict but a very kind and gentle person.

Sir Edward's daughter, Miss Molly Mann, founded the 1st Thelveton Troop of Boy Scouts and became their Scout Mistress. Sir Edward had four sons. One was killed in action in the First World War and in his memory Sir Edward built three bungalows for the use of the elderly. The gardens at the front of these bungalows were always kept tidy by the Hall Gardeners. Sir Edward was also the proud father of the Middlesex and England batsman, Frank Mann, who was renowned for his ability to knock the bowling for six more times than most. Major Edgar Mann was Sir Edward's second eldest son and he farmed in the village of Earl Soham along the same lines as his father at Thelveton. They became friendly rivals at the County Shows with their herds of dairy shorthorn cows. John was Sir Edward's eldest son and they were constant companions – it was very rare to see one without the other.

I have described the Mann family at some length because the life of the whole village revolved around The Hall. Life seemed to radiate from its walls.

Sir Edward himself was a partner and chairman of the London-based brewery 'Mann Crossman & Paulin Limited'.

Chapter 3

The Village Workers

Eli Aldous	– Cowman	– Manor Farm
Simon Aldous	– Farm Foreman	– Tolegate & Manor Farms
Walter Aldous	– Groom	– The Manor House
H Baker	– Ploughman	– Grange Farm
Mrs Buck	– Midwife and Layer Out at time of death	
T Coulson	– Painter	– Thelveton Estate
A Cox	– Head Groom	– Thelveton Hall
P Ellis	– General Labourer	– Thelveton Hall
W Farington	– Farm Foreman	– Grange Farm
Albert Foreman	– Labourer	– Grange Farm
George Foreman	– Engine Driver	– All Farms
Joe Foreman	– Labourer	– Grange Farm
Edgar Gipson	– Cowman	– Tolegate Farm
G Gipson	– Cowman	– Tolegate Farm
A W Gipson Snr.	– Head Gardener	– Thelveton Hall
William Gipson	– Head Cowman	– Manor Farm
William Gipson Jnr.	– Gardener	– Thelveton Hall
A Knights	– Butler	– Thelveton Hall
D Leeder	– Farm Worker	– Grange Farm
E Leeder	– Gardener	– The Rectory
Joe Leeder	– Pigman	– Grange Farm
L Leeder	– Labourer	– Grange Farm
P Leeder	– Gamekeeper's Assistant	– Thelveton Estate
F Meadows	– Shepherd	– Thelveton Estate
Bob Mills	– Horseman	– Grange Farm

G Mills	– Carpenter	– Grange Farm
Ted Mills	– Horseman	– Grange Farm
W Moore	– Carpenter	– Tolegate Farm
William (Diddy) Moore	– Engine Driver	– Thelveton Estate
Fred Moss	– Horseman	– Grange Farm
Alfred Mullenger	– Cowman	– Grange Farm
Clem Mullenger	– Head Horseman (Later years)	– Grange Farm
Elija Mullenger	– Head Horseman (Earlier years)	– Grange Farm
H Mullenger	– Cowman	– Grange Farm
Rhuban Mullenger	– Head Cowman	– Grange Farm
R Neale	– Head Gamekeeper	– Thelveton Estate
F Noble	– Gardener	– Thelveton Hall
William Nunn	– Gardener	– Thelveton Hall
W Nunn	– Gamekeeper	– Thelveton Estate
J Oiris	– Gamekeeper	– Thelveton Estate
A Philpot	– General Labourer	– Grange Farm
G Philpot	– Labourer	– Grange Farm
W Philpot	– Assistant Gamekeeper	– Thelveton Estate
J Pope	– Labourer	– Grange Farm
J Pope Snr.	– Horseman	– Manor Farm
A Potter	– Horseman	– Manor Farm
J Potter	– Gamekeeper	– Thelveton Estate
C Race	– Horseman	– Manor Farm
Herbert Rudd	– Horseman	– Tolegate Farm
William Ruddock	– Labourer	– Brick Kiln Farm
William Sargent	– Chef	– Thelveton Hall
George Saunders	– Head Carpenter	– Thelveton Estate
P Self	– Cowman	– Tolegate Farm
G Smith	– Gamekeeper	– Thelveton Estate
A Talbot	– Dairyman	– Grange Farm
F Talbot	– Horseman	– Tolegate Farm
Jack Talbot Snr.	– Woodman	– Thelveton Estate
Jack Talbot Jnr.	– Assistant Carpenter	– Tolegate Farm
Joe Talbot	– Gardener	– Grange Farm House
J Talbot	– Woodman	– Thelveton Estate

S Talbot (the writer)	– Gardener	– Thelveton Hall
R Warnes	– Engine Driver also Assistant Scout Master	– Thelveton Hall
G Watson	– Gamekeeper	– Thelveton Estate

These are the true names of all the characters in the village in those early days. At some time in my life they have all played a part – some minor and some major – in keeping the village a smooth-running community.

Thelveton is divided into two parts: the Norwich to Ipswich main road which takes in two estate farms – the Tolegate and the Manor; while at the other end of the Thelveton Hall drive is Grange Farm with all its cottages close round. The Rectory is situated at that end too. The Right Reverend Johnson was the Rector at that time. The church is situated in the middle of some fields close to Grange Farm but was, and still is, a lonely place which we youngsters used to shun if possible as our elders seemed to enjoy telling us eerie stories of people jumping out of the graves and chasing us. We had such vivid imaginations that we thought it true and to make matters worse, in those days glass domes with artificial flowers were a common sight in churchyards and when the sun shone on the domes they looked exceedingly frightening from a distance.

Back in my early school days I soon began to realize what a lot there was to learn about what was going on in the outside world. There was a war on and the things we were told were hardly believable because there was no radio and the telephone was practically non-existent. Every bit of news was by word of mouth or from the newspaper. We hardly knew what went on in the next village – there seemed to be an invisible screen between each village – until our fathers went to the pub or our mothers went to a funeral in a neighbouring village. Mind you, some women liked going to funerals and would often walk six miles to one. They could hardly get home quick enough to pass on a bit of scandal. My mother was one such person, as a matter of fact I cannot ever remember seeing her out of black clothes. All my young life she would love to come home and relate to us over the tea table what a lovely funeral it had been and who had been there.

Chapter 4

War and The Foot Soldier

'There's a Zeppelin about, I can hear it!' mother shouted. It was the middle of the night and I was hastily dragged from my bed and made to sit on the bottom stair with mother shaking on the next stair. We listened to the throb of the engines overhead and a peculiar swishing noise as the Zeppelin passed over. Then all of a sudden 'crump crump crump' came the sound of explosions quite near. We found out the next day as the whole village gathered in a group talking: 'Them Germans nearly had us last night. They dropped their bombs at Billingford and killed some horses.' What happened, as was found out afterwards, was the Zeppelin had a long wire hanging from its underside at the end of which hung a large basket in which an observer would be placed to act as a lookout for the airman above. In the ship was a field telephone which was connected to the basket which was riding very quietly so the lookout could hear the slightest noise below. It was thought that on this occasion he heard the sound of galloping hooves in the field below and thought they were military horses, perhaps with a regiment of troops, hence the bombing. It has to be remembered that during the First World War nothing but horses were used as the army was not mechanized.

The next day was to bring this point home to me as early in the morning someone said 'We hear there are thousands of troops on the move, going to the front. We might see them going past here'. Sure enough this was proved to be true. I don't know how the informer got to know but before long we could hear a military band playing in the distance. The sound seemed to get ever nearer and we country folk began to tremble with anticipation of what we were about to see. As the sound got nearer we could hear the jingle of the tackle of hundreds of horses and then the steady clump, clump of thousands of marching feet, a sound I shall never

11

forget. As the British Army came into view our hearts nearly stopped. Never shall I forget the sight of those swinging arms, just like a machine. To this day I can see that long column which seemed to reach from Dickleburgh to Scole without a break – some two miles. The Limbers with their guns all shining like new; the Officers with their white braids on their shoulders; cap badges glinting in the sunlight; everyone with their legs wrapped in neat putties. All the men wore shoulder badges made of real brass. To see this on our own doorstep so to speak was unheard of. At the rear of this vast column of troops came the wagons containing the tents of which there were hundreds. Large tents for the mess etc. and smaller ones for the troops. There were loads of hay for the horses and sacks of tent pegs, all being pulled by mules of which the Army had thousands. After they had gone it all seemed like a dream to us but the proof we had of them being there was the trail of horse manure which seemed to stretch for miles! This event in our lives was to be repeated many times before the war ended.

Chapter 5

Learning the Village Ways

As I began to learn this and that, I soon found out what was right and what was wrong and all about the laws of the village. The first thing we had drilled into us, even as infants, was to respect the Squire and his family at all times. The boys were taught to salute properly, the girls shown how to curtsey. Then we were told how to address them if ever we were in their company. We were always to say 'Yes Sir Edward' or 'No Sir Edward' and to remember we must never speak first, and only speak if spoken to. We soon learned that all game such as pheasants, partridges and hares were not ours – they belonged to the Hall. The Squire employed keepers to look after them and if anyone was caught taking game, severe punishment could be expected. In very serious cases of poaching, one might expect to be turned out of one's cottage.

Rabbits were very plentiful and were known as the poor man's meat; while you were not allowed to wander around catching rabbits, you were not questioned if you caught one in your garden or on the land of the farmer who sublet the farm from the Squire. Most of the land in Thelveton was farmed by Grange Farm; the other two farms – Tolegate and Manor, were sublet to John Symonds. Tolegate Farm was where my father worked as a horseman. We lived almost opposite the farm and I can remember my father starting work each day at 4 a.m. to feed his horses, ready for the hard work in the day to come. I can see the shadows of his legs reflected on the ceiling as I lay in bed as he walked to work past our window carrying his oil lantern. There was no electricity then, not even a torch, so everything was lit by candle or oil lamp. Very dangerous was the candle; if you read by candlelight and held it too close the slightest puff of air would blow the flame several inches and I have known a comic which was being read to catch fire. I once remember a girl with long hair experience

13

the horror of seeing her hair on fire. Fortunately someone was near to hand and put a cushion over it so very little damage was done. As for the oil lamps, these were even more dangerous. It has to be remembered that in those days everyone had long tablecloths on their tables at all times and the oil lamp would easily topple over; we children had to be very careful when playing not to knock the lamp over. However, I can honestly say that throughout my childhood days and up to the time I was married we never had electricity and not once did I know of any serious accident with an oil lamp.

The men who worked on the farm all had their own lamps and it was quite a sight early mornings, and early evenings in the Winter, to see lamps shining with yellow light all over the farm. The cowmen with their lamps, the horsemen with theirs, the pigmen with theirs.

Lanterns would also be carried by the labourers as they were busy setting rat traps all around their properties to try to keep the rat population down. There were great numbers of rats everywhere. As every house kept chickens and most kept pigs and large numbers of rabbits were kept in hutches, this encouraged the rats, so gin traps were used everywhere where rats frequented. They had to be sprung during the day for fear of catching pheasants and the like. The traps were very cruel and many a poor cat had to be destroyed after being caught in a trap, as cats roamed at night like the rats. As children we soon learned how to kill rats and even at a very early age I would chase out with a lantern at night when I heard a rat screaming. I knew from this that it was in a trap and if left long enough it would bite its own leg off at the point where it was caught in the trap, likewise its tail, too, if the tail had sprung the trap. I had a special stick I used to kill the rats with and I was really proud to come in to my father and mother and say 'I got him'. Father would then go out and reset the trap as it was too strong a spring for me to press down. I was only 8 or 9 years old at that time. Sometimes rats would get in the roof of the house and we could lay in bed and hear them chewing away at the beams and running across the floor over the ceiling above our heads. We found out they had climbed inside the drainpipe to gain entry from under the tiles and we had to stuff the drainpipe with wire netting to prevent this.

As well as the rats, every house without exception was often overrun with mice, so we all had mousetraps and it was not unusual to catch five or six in a day but still they would come as they bred very quickly.

When I was about 4½ years old, my mother's youngest sister was suffering with consumption (tuberculosis) and was slowly dying. She was only 28 and there was no cure for that illness in those days. She was in a bed in our front room and as she slowly got worse I was told not to go in and see her as mother did not want me to see her in that state. When she died, my father fixed a button (lock) on top of the door into the room so I should not see the coffin. Each night I was taken out of the back door and round to the front of the house to go in the front door to go to bed. This was very skilfully carried out because it was several days before I realized my auntie was no longer there.

In the village, as was usual in most villages, we had a midwife and 'layer out of corpses' – ours was a Mrs Buck. When anyone died she would be sent for, any time of day or night. If it was thought someone was going to die, the neighbours would listen for Mrs Buck going past on the way to do her duties. She had a long black skirt which scraped along the ground so she could easily be heard as she went past. If it was wet and muddy, she collected an ounce or two of mud on the bottom of her skirt and this made it very difficult for her to walk in comfort, so she would hold her skirt up a few inches. If she thought anyone was looking, she would drop it to the ground again as no-one was allowed to glimpse a tiny bit of ankle.

The most important thing I was to learn was the importance of a Sunday, when no one was allowed to work except the stockmen who fed the animals. The rest of us had to go to church or chapel if possible. The children were almost forced to attend Sunday School and anyone over the age of nine had to join the church choir if they could sing!!

So, by the time I was 6 or 7 years old, I had learned quite a lot of what was required of me in the parish!

Chapter 6

'Where's Mine?'

As time passed by I grew to be aware of what life was all about. Even as a small boy I used to wonder about all sorts of things, especially why there were so many cows in the meadow and why they disappeared out of sight every night only to return in the morning. I soon found out they had to be milked because as soon as I was able to do a few jobs I was expected to go to the farm each morning, which was a quarter of a mile away, armed with two or three milk cans. Each can held a quart and I had to collect the milk for the old people living in the Memorial Cottages. Milk was ld a pint and skimmed milk ½d; at the end of the week I was paid 3d (1.25p) which was a lot of money for a child to earn in those days. Several children did this for various people before going to school.

There were also the large flocks of sheep, around 500, which used to be cared for by Mr Meadows. They would often pass by our gate on their way to fresh pastures, with dogs barking and the shepherd shouting. While this was to become an almost everyday scene, I soon realized my father must be doing something out there. Likewise all the other men who seemed to be going this way and that, carrying strange things which, of course, were their tools of trade, which were many and varied. To me this was something I felt I must be a part of. As I grew up, my father soon taught me what he had been doing all this time – the art of being a horseman. Horses are wonderful creatures and it was not long before I knew all the horses on the farm by name and they learned to trust me even though I was only small, aged about 10. When, to my mother's horror, I first led a great shire horse pulling a tumbril past our house, my father was told in no uncertain terms that night how she disapproved of him allowing me to be in charge of such a large animal. He said 'He (meaning me) won't get hurt, he had old Moggy, she won't stand on his feet.' However, I noticed I was not allowed to pass our house again with a horse for some years but I still managed to use her around the farm buildings, carting beet, chaff and muck. I loved doing this and I felt like a man.

I must have felt like a man when I was about 4 or 5 years old, as the following little story will confirm. Every Sunday night in the summertime, our parents used to go for long walks, mostly over the footpaths and always finishing at a pub, taking us with them. In those days a child was not allowed in the bars, so most pubs had a private room where children could play while their parents enjoyed a drink. Well, this night, we finished up at Dickleburgh Crown and, as there were no other children in the private room, I was allowed to stand quietly in the passage between the bars where the grown-ups were all busy drinking. My father ordered a pint for himself and a glass of stout for my mother. The landlord was busy serving and while all this was going on I shouted in a very loud voice 'Where's mine?'. There was a moment's silence, then the whole place erupted in loud laughter. It tickled the adults' sense of humour so much and the words 'Where's mine?' lived with me for years afterwards. Mr Steggles, who used to be a bell ringer and was always cycling by our house to various churches, would always shout 'Where's mine?' if he saw me in the garden.

Chapter 7

Farm Life As It Was

Farm life, as I remember it from 1916 onwards, was truly the work of nature and the men were the executioners of this wonderful work. These men knew when to plough and how to grow certain crops and what a job they made of it. Their furrows were dead straight, likewise when they drilled the corn it was in perfect rows. They were so proud of their work and the work of others – they would walk or cycle miles to see other men's work. In the pubs on a Sunday dinner time one would often say to another 'You think you can plough? Well, you want to go and look at the ten acres down the lane back of the church and see Bob's bit of plough-ing.' Likewise, when the stackyard was filled with stacks after harvest – sometimes there would be as many as 28 stacks in one yard – another voice would say 'Anyone want to see how stacks should be built? Well, go you and look at Ted's, there's no legs there.' (Legs are wooden props used to hold a stack up if it is badly built.) Then these old boys would down their pints and perhaps detour several miles on their way home just to look at someone's work. Sometimes they would have a bet who could plough the straightest and hence every year a ploughing match would be staged on one of the farms. Ploughmen from miles around would descend on this field and draw furrows in competition with each other for the first prize of a copper kettle. Bob Reeve, licensee of the local Greyhound pub, would be there supplying refreshments. Some of us boys would have a sip or two but were careful who was looking! Now and again there would be two furrows dead straight and these had to be re-drawn. The loser would be only ¼" out, such was their skill.

Most farms had their own threshing machine tackle consisting of an engine, drum and strawpitcher. On our farm we had two portable engines which we boys, and even some of the girls, thought were wonderful machines. We all looked forward to them being used in the winter when the great stacks were threshed, thus releasing the hundreds of mice and rats concealed in the stack bottom which was exposed after a day's work and would be alive with vermin. We used to have all our sticks ready in the school porch for when it was time to go at 3.45 p.m., this would be about the right time, if we ran fast enough to the farm, to have a good hour's sport as we called it, killing as many rats as we could when they found it hard to escape due to the wire netting which had been placed around before the work started. With the men's help, and perhaps a dog someone had brought, over 200 rats would sometimes be accounted for and hundreds of mice. Bean stacks were the most prolific for rats. We thought this nothing unusual and could see no fear, though a rat can be very dangerous if cornered.

Now to tell you a bit more about the work these men had to do before threshing. The whole thing had to be set; what I mean by this is that the drum had to be in the correct position. This may sound easy but was not, as the drum had to be drawn into position by horses in a stackyard of mud and stones. These poor horses were often beaten until they pulled this great drum at a gallop, because if they stopped they would never get started again. The ground was so soft I have seen the horses with their bellies almost on the ground but with their willingness to pull they always managed it. When the drum was in position, on a mark the engine driver had made with his foot, the horseman would shout 'Whoa' and you could always be sure this would be in the correct position. Then the engine had

Farm workers at Rushall.

to be pulled to its correct drive position, this was heavy but not as bad as the drum. Again the engine driver, Diddy Moore, would make a mark with his foot for the wheel to come to which, when achieved, would be correct for driving the drum. Setting the strawpitcher was easy compared to the other machines.

On the next morning the men would begin to arrive: one to pull the thatch off, and Diddy to get his fire going for the steam. This would be at about 6.30 a.m. Perhaps there would be a couple of inches of ice on the water tank which was next to the engine, and the air would be freezing cold, maybe with little sleet flurries, which all adds up to a very cold morning. The first thing some of the men would do would be to break the ice on the tank, then, taking their jackets off, roll up their shirt sleeves. They would plunge their arms into the water up to their elbows for a few minutes and then give their arms a brisk rub with a chaff bag until their circulation returned. This, they reckoned, helped them to never feel the cold any more all day. Threshing is a dirty job, particularly for the person on the chaff box, filling chaff bags from the box all day and throwing the coulter into the strawpitcher with a fork. This was the worst job in a day's threshing, especially if a bean stack was being threshed. Mostly a boy just starting work would be put on this job, or someone who perhaps was not quite up to the standard required for the more delicate job of weighing the corn or building the new strawstack.

Farmers were a mixed lot. Some were known for their generosity while others were known for their meanness. One miserly farmer used to hire a set of tackle to thresh his corn. He was asked by the man in charge of the threshing gang if he, the farmer, would pay the boy in the gang the same as the others, as he was very strong and worked just as hard. The pay was 5 shillings for men and 2 shillings and 6 pence for boys for a day's work from 7 a.m. until 4 p.m. Then sometimes the men would have to walk 7 or 8 miles home. The farmer said no as rates were rates and as the boy was 14 years old he would only get the 2s 6d due to him. This farmer had a novel way of settling up the day's pay. He would stand all the half crowns (2s 6d) in a long row on the gate leading into the stackyard: 2 each for the men, one for the boy. The man in charge who had asked for extra said to the boy 'Keep you close to me, we will go first.' Everyone had to help themselves to their two halfcrowns on the way out. When they got to the gate, the man kicked it and all the halfcrowns went flying. He said to the boy 'Pick you two up' and that was how he made sure the boy got paid for doing a man's work. Just a little story to show there were some quick-thinking men about in those days.

Chapter 8

The Harvest

Every field had a name and as youngsters we soon learned the names off by heart and would get to know which field our fathers were working in, as we had to take meals to them during the school holidays. The women-folk would often go and take their wonderful baskets of hot food to their menfolk. The aroma when the pie dishes of meat puddings were exposed to the air was never to be forgotten. There was the sight of sometimes 15 men siting on the brow of a ditch, all eating, with the horses stamping their feet and eating lucerne close by, with sprigs of elder stuck in their head harnesses to keep the flies away. There were thousands of flies and every now and then 'I got stung by a blasted wasp' the voice of an angry worker would say. 'That's the smell of your runner beans,' another voice would shout. 'Runner beans always seems to attract wasps.' Everyone had to watch each mouthful in case he got a wasp in his mouth. The same trouble would be repeated a few minutes later when the home-brewed beer was uncorked, as the smell of this seemed to draw large numbers of wasps. There was much swishing of caps and stamping of feet and the air was filled with the sound of choice words which, to my ears, sounded awful as at school we were warned never to use such words or the devil would get us. He would have a catch here, I thought. However, I soon learned to live with this, as I soon found out that outbreaks such as this were commonplace when things did not always go as planned.

Before all the carting could take place, the corn had to be cut. In the very early days this was done by hand but by the time I took an active interest in the workings on the farm the reaper had been invented, which was called a Sailer. This consisted of a platform with a moving knife at the front which worked off the drive wheel which in turn was activated by the movement of the machine being drawn by two horses. At the same

21

time another flat plate attached to the gearing revolved to which four sails were attached which could be adjusted to the height of the corn. These were very ingenious and interesting to watch, as one sail would sweep the standing corn onto the moving blades then leap almost straight up on its journey round. The next sail would push corn off the platform at the back where it had to be tied into convenient bundles. The man on the machine experienced a frightening sensation as these great sails came straight at him with regularity only to do a peculiar jump over his head as they continued on their journey down, to repeat the performance over and over again. This machine was never liked much but it was better than cutting by hand. It was especially useful to cut laid corn. It was being whispered that they would soon have a machine that would cut and tie corn all by itself.

'Impossible,' most of them would say. 'Who heard of a machine that could cut and tie all in one operation?'

'Can't be done,' one said.

'You wait and see,' another said. He was always a bit more learned than most of us. 'Things are on the move,' he carried on, looking up into the sky as if seeking divine guidance. 'This here machine what cut corn now is only the start, you will see if you live long enough. Better ones will follow. They've got steam ships now, when they used to have sails. Old sailors never believed that anything would be better than wind but it was; the same here. There will be better machines than this and now they can make one, they will make anything.' Having exhausted himself with such a long bit of knowledge, he continued eating a large shortcake. He was renowned for eating these large shortcakes and his wife would always pride herself on the size of them: they were enormous. The men all went back to work and the farm was running smoothly again.

I am describing the machines used at some length so the reader gets the feeling we had in those times of wonder. As, believe you me, we lived in the age of discovery in the true sense of the word and the conversation would always include the question 'Have you heard?' to which someone would reply 'They will never do away with horses' and so each day passed with the same question and the same answer. One day a man cycled into the farmyard from Diss saying 'You want to look out together they will soon have something what will do the work of your old horses.' To which one of the listeners said 'Git you back to Diss with yar yarns that'll be a long while afore they git some machine to work through the beet like a hoss.' To this the man replied 'It won't be long now,' and off he went.

When the corn had been cut, the sheaves were carted to the farm to be
stacked. It was a carefully planned operation. There would be one wagon
in the field being loaded with another empty one standing by. Two men
would be loading, this was a job for experts and the best loaders were
always chosen for this work. Two men would pitch the sheaves up to the
loader when they had finished two shocks (about 14 sheeves) from each
side of the wagon. One of the men would shout 'Hold tight'. The men on
the wagon would do just that and the horses would walk forward to the
next block of shocks. There would also be the shout of 'Water furrow'
which meant the wagon was about to cross a water furrow which was
common in all arable fields. The men would renew their hold on the load
which by this time would be getting quite high – 10 to 12 feet. It would
then be ready to rope. Two ropes would be thrown up. One at the front and
one at the rear, the snoose end would be thrown down which would be
attached to hooks under the wagon. The men would then slide down
clutching the now tight rope onto the ground. They would stand back and
survey their handiwork and give instructions on how much to pull the load
upright before making it secure. The load would then be safe to make its
journey to the farm, which sometimes was nearly ¾ of a mile away. The

Elevator (worked by horse underneath).

field known as the 'Aldecar' was one such as this. The bigger boys would sometimes be allowed to do the job of driving away (as it was called). I loved this job when I was old enough to do it. The load left the field and was met half-way home by another empty wagon. The drivers would exchange over and this load would continue on its way to the farm where another cart was being unloaded on to an elevator driven by a horse which was connected to the works underneath the machine. This was quite simple really but fairly hard work and boring to the horse and driver. He had to go round and round all day long, attached to a pole which drove the works which, in turn, carried sheaves of corn being unloaded off the wagon to the newly built corn stacks which in themselves were a work of art. The stacker would be very proud of his work and great care went into building the stack some 20 feet long and 10 feet wide. Sizes varied according to how much each sort of corn was going on each stack. A 10 or 12 acre field could be put on to one stack if care was taken in its construction.

The harvest continued and we went back to school after the four weeks holiday. We always helped on the farm as we had to have a holiday to coincide with the harvest.

Chapter 9

Steam and Prayers

As soon as the harvest was over, the fields had to be broken up (cultivated) to chit the corn which had been left on the ground and to kill the weeds. The summers were nearly always very hot and consequently the ground got extremely dry. Being heavy soil, no horse could pull the cultivators, so the steam ploughs and cultivators were called in to do the job. What a treat it was for us children to see these massive giants, weighing 20 tons each, invade our farms for a few weeks. It was a truly wonderful sight to see these great engines with their quarter mile of steel cable under their massive bellies standing at each end of the field pulling the cultivator (plough) backwards and forwards with the cable attached to a huge revolving drum. The engines themselves made a terrific noise which was very musical to our ears. These engines seemed alive; they would work from daybreak at about 5 a.m. until 10 p.m. or as long as daylight permitted. There were five men of which one was the foreman who rode on the plough and another was the cook. They had their own sleeping van where they would all sleep and eat. Coal and water had to be brought to the engine all the time they were working. To signal their need for one or the other, one whistle would be given for water and two whistles for coal.

A farm labourer would be with the set of steam engines for the period they were at work. A very quiet horse had to be used to bring the water and coal as the engines were very frightening to animals especially when they hissed as the coal or water was unloaded, because the horse would be standing very close.

When these giants passed on to the next farm, we youngsters would pretend to be steam engines and would imitate them. One of us would stand at each end of the meadow with a long piece of string attached to a boy in between, who was supposed to be the plough. So we passed many happy hours, such was the attraction of steam.

It must be remembered that whilst all this was going on the rest of the farm carried on in full swing with the many and varied jobs continuing.

I was at school, still wondering 'Why?' about everything around me and as I grew older I felt more responsible. At the age of 9 I was told I must take a voice test to qualify for the church choir. I hoped I would fail but no, I passed, and then had to attend choir practice every week which meant a journey across the fields to our lonely church. I dreaded this because of the stories I had heard, but with a crowd of about five others it was not so bad.

At that time a Miss Eaton was the organist and the Revd Johnson was our rector. In my later years at the church, they were succeeded by Miss Winifred Neal as organist and the Revd Unthank as rector.

At Christmas all the girls in the choir received a dress length from the Squire, while the boys received a new suit. These were called Sunday clothes and were only worn on 'high days' and Sundays. The 'high days' were special occasions: we dare not wear them willy nilly in case they got stained, as we always had to look smart on a Sunday.

Harvest Thanksgiving service was the highlight of the church and village life and was attended by every person in the parish: they were expected to attend. To hear the rich voices of the men who we never previously knew could sing was a sound I will always remember. The collection was much appreciated by the rector as this was the one day in the year when the collection was for him. We had to put 2d in instead of the usual 1d. This practice stopped when the Tithe Law was abolished a few years later. Every rector had the use of a field or meadow from the Squire or farmer and everything grown on this field was to help the rector augment his wage. This was called a tithe.

When anyone passed away, the deceased was always announced by the ringing of the church bell – one ring for each year of life. This was done twelve hours after the death had taken place and there would be a one minute interval between each ring so it took a long time to conclude the practice if a person was very old. The village people used to wait outside to count the strokes of the bell so they could say to one another 'I knew old so and so was older than he said, I counted the bells.' The sexton was responsible for ringing the bells. He would pull the bell rope, then walk the full length of the church and back at a slowly measured pace; this would take exactly one minute. It could be a very lonely job, especially if it had to be done at night with no electricity, just an oil lamp, and this often happened as the twelve hours after death was strictly observed. The grave for the deceased would also be dug by the sexton, who had to dig it after working hours, with the faithful oil lamp for company, as the farmer would not let him lose any working hours during the day. He would be paid ls (5p) for the job by the undertaker. He would also have a wooden frame of the size of the grave which had to be dug – if this would fit the grave after it was finished, then the coffin would go in. This had to be done, as most of the men could neither read nor write, having left school at the age of seven to nine. Coffins were left in the house of the deceased as there were no funeral parlours. We children were frightened to go anywhere near a house where a body was laying. Our parents used to tell us the most gruesome stories about dead people that we were glad when the burial had taken place!

Chapter 10

The Self-Binder Arrives

I was nine years old, fully aware of the happenings of the village and what the people did. Our neighbours were perhaps the closest friends we had, Alfred and his wife and two children; he was the horseman at Manor Farm. A very musical man, he would often have what he called a concert with the children on a Sunday morning. He would say 'If it's a concert you want, you will have one,' and he would sing the latest songs of the day, which sounded good to us next door, as he had a good voice. Little things like that all helped to make life enjoyable.

At harvest time that year a relation of the family came to stay, with their son Frankie. He and I played together and as he was a Londoner he knew very little about farm life. It was left to me to keep him out of mischief and not allow him to frighten the horses. One day we were walking around the ten acres near the stackyard with our sticks, poking in the grass at the edge of the field trying to disturb a rabbit, when we spotted a large rabbit hole. Frankie said 'Poke them in the hole Sidney, a rabbit will come out.' We were soon running for our lives as, instead of a rabbit appearing, hundreds of angry wasps chased us all the way back to the farm stackyard, stinging us all the time. We screamed and screamed and had soon attracted the attention of the men who were working and the women who had just arrived with their dinners. Fortunately my mother was there and she soon stripped us both naked and removed the remaining wasps with her hands, getting stung in the process. Some of the men also got stung as there were plenty of wasps still flying around. There was much swearing and cap swotting. I got most of the blame and was told I should have known better. We were then covered all over with a 'blue bag' which mother had hastily gone to the nearest house to fetch (this was a sound remedy for stings). We were stung on almost every inch of our bodies and were ill for several days but I think it cured us from poking into strange holes.

It was at this time that the foreman came to see my father to inform him he was going to have the new-fangled self-binder to use and someone would come from away to teach him to use it. He soon found there was a lot to learn. The great day arrived and a brand new 'Massey Harris' machine was brought from the station (everything was delivered by rail in those days). The knowledgeable man was from a well-known engineering firm and he soon explained in a very educational way 'How this here thing works. It not only cuts the corn but ties it up as well, then throws it out at the side in sheaves for you to pick up.' After a lot of explaining how to thread the needle with string (the hardest part) he departed. To this day I marvel at how the machine was invented in those early days of engineering.

'I told you so,' a loud voice said. 'I knew it would come.' This was from the man who had previously predicted this very machine would be made. It was on the first day when the binder was tried out and several men were allowed to witness this marvel of engineering. To the simple country folk it was wonderful and some would wonder what would be next. This first machine was so successful that another was obtained for Manor Farm, this time it was an 'Albion'. A third binder was obtained for

The Self-Binder.

After the field is cut . . . Rear view of binder and workers with the catch of rabbits.

Grange Farm – a 'McCormick' and there was much arguing in the pubs as to which was the better machine and, more to the point, who was able to use it best? There were always friendly arguments in the pubs as to who made the best job of their work – there was such pride in what they did.

Chapter 11

The Coming of the Wireless

In the 1920s we first heard about the wireless. Few people believed it even when they did hear it. We first knew about it when a friend of my mother who lived in the next village said to her 'We have got a wireless Libby, people speak to us from London through the air, there are no wires, only from the apple tree. It scares me a bit. Come and bring Fred (my Dad) and Sidney next week.' When mother told us about the invitation we got very excited and could hardly wait for the great day to arrive. When it did, we all had to wear our Sunday clothes as this was a special occasion. When we arrived at the house, Mrs Hammond was very excited and told us there was a wireless aerial from the apple tree to the house which picked up the sound. We went inside and all our eyes were fixed to this oblong box which stood near the window with earphones attached. Mr Hammond explained that he had to fiddle with a 'cat's whisker' before it would work. I thought for a moment he had got to play with the whiskers of their pet cat lying on the hearth, such was my ignorance of these things at the time. He put on the earphones and said 'Ahh! I have got something here – yes, here you are, have a listen.' With that he handed the earphones to my mother who nearly jumped out of her shoes when, as she said afterwards, a voice from nowhere had said 'This is London 2LO speaking.' My father nearly did the same thing when he was handed the earphones a few moments later. I couldn't wait for my turn to come, but come it did when, instead of handing me the earphones, Mr Hammond said that if we got a big cooking bowl and lay the earphones in that and listened we would all be able to hear at the same time. He was right, we could all hear a faint but clear voice talking to us from London. I have often wondered if that was perhaps the very first loudspeaker. As we walked the mile or so home, this experience at hearing a voice from London was all we could talk about. I could hardly sleep that night thinking of what I had to tell the school children the next day. I had to write an essay on what I had seen and heard so the school teacher could read it out to the other children. Such was the importance of the discovery of the wireless that everyone was talking about it and I felt very important and privileged to have been the very first child from our village to have experienced the real thing.

As time went by, almost everyone managed to have a crystal set. This required a 50-foot aerial leading from a pole in the garden, usually put in an apple tree to conceal the pole so the boss would not be able to see it when going past, otherwise he might think he was paying too much. Consequently there were raids on all the woods for miles around for good straight wireless poles. These raids would be after dark for obvious reasons!

Such was the fear of the boss that men used to be afraid to smoke. Clay pipes were the pipes used for a crafty smoke because they could be broken off at the desired length so as not to be seen sticking out from a distance. They were known as 'nose warmers' and were very useful when ploughing as they could be lit in the knowledge that they could not be seen from the gate. But the workers would keep a wary eye on the gate for the farmer to appear. If he did, they would spit their pipe out into the furrow without stopping the plough and would make a mark on the newly ploughed soil with their foot so they could retrieve the pipe later when the farmer had gone. This was another instance of the farmer thinking he was paying them too much.

I was doing more and more jobs on the farm, chiefly with the horses as all our lives revolved around these animals. Every man talked about little else but horses, cows, sheep and pigs; consequently when any of the animals were ill most men knew how to deal with the complaint themselves as there were no vets about, only self-taught ones.

I remember one day I heard my father say he would have to do something about Bowler's tooth – Bowler was the horse. I nearly fainted when I heard my father say 'We shall have to knock it out with a hammer and chisel, we will do it on Sunday afternoon'. I knew the poor horse was off its food through this rotten tooth and would soon have had to be put down when it could no longer eat so I realized my father had to do something about it. The dreaded day arrived and in the morning I watched my father mix up a strange lotion in a jar. This, I found out afterwards, was a secret mixture known only to horsemen. When he was ready for the big job, he put some of the lotion in Blower's ear and near its nose which sent the horse into a doze. He then prised its mouth open and 'bang' the job was done. The horse recovered quickly and was soon eating again.

I add this to my story to show how much those men were the masters of their trade, even knowing the right remedies to give their animals, though the workers could barely read or write properly. They knew that everything had its use – even the root of the deadly nightshade was used with other ingredients to make a horse's coat shine.

Chapter 12

Snow Time

The old people would say 'If there is a green Christmas there will be a fat churchyard.' Occasionally there was a mild winter but most years winter would be heralded in December by very sharp frosts with ice six inches thick in no time at all, which pleased us youngsters. We would soon be sliding on every pond in the village. Dickleburgh Moor would be frozen over for about six to eight weeks. Some years there would be ice skating and a lot of people used to come from miles around, most of them on bicycles and some in carts driven by horses but very few in cars. The arrival of the skater was popular with the boys and young men in the village who would borrow their mothers' brooms and sweep wide paths through the snow for the skaters, who would give some very good tips. The village shellfish dealer would set up his stall on the ice, selling cockles at ld a saucer. I remember one boy skating round with his broom, smoking two cigarettes at the same time saying 'I can afford two packets now I have done well in tips.' I still fail to see the logic in that!

One night at teatime the foreman came to see my father, saying 'By the look of the sky tonight there's a lot of snow coming. I want you to get out early with your horses and pick up the snow plough at Elwoods Corner and clear the roads so the milk can be got to the station.' That was very important as all the milk from the country had to go by the milk train to London every day at 8 a.m. My father had to go to the crossroads where the plough had been left since last winter. Similarly, other ploughs were left at crossroads ready for winter. Each village cleared the roads which passed through it. My father or whoever did it started on the boundary with Scole and cleared the road to the boundary with Dickleburgh – a distance of two miles. This operation would be repeated by other villages, who would link up with each other so the main roads would be clear all the way to the railway station. Thus the milk could get through to London in time. After the main roads were clear, the horses would be given a rest and another pair would take over with other horsemen. The clearing of all the side roads would then take place. Sometimes it would snow all day and the same procedure would be repeated so the milk could get through again for the milk train at night.

In order that the Squire could catch his train to London, the horses which pulled his carriage had corkings screwed into their shoes to stop them from slipping.

We children had to go to school whatever the weather. The school caretaker was a lady who looked after and kept the school clean and lit the 'Tortoise' stove fire. She would be up very early clearing the school paths of snow and fetching pails of water from the well (no taps then!) This was very hard work for very little pay. She was also expected to scrub the whole school floor on her hands and knees. It was a very rough floor, full of knots in the wood, and worn very badly due to the wearing for years and years of hobnail boots. There were sticks to chop and coke to fetch in every day during the winter months. Another of her school duties was to look after the Head Teacher's house which adjoined the school. This was all in addition to looking after her own house and family. Yes, these were very hard times for some.

Another chore which went with the running of the school was the twice weekly emptying of the school lavatory pails as of course we had no flush toilets then. This was done by a willing pair of hands – one of a large family. He used to do this job late at night and receive the princely sum of £2 every three months. He used to say he got the value of two pints of beer – 8d – for every emptying.

The snow seemed to be with us for ever. Everywhere was deathly quiet: remember there were no tractors, lorries or cars to fill the air with noise. Even the birds were quiet. All that could be heard in those days was the distant shout of a stockman calling some poor creature an awkward 'B', or some poor pig meeting its doom at the butcher's, a sound I never liked to hear. Although we lived with them all the time, the coming of the winter snow amplified these sounds out of all proportion. The sound I did like to hear was that of the engine powering the threshing drum on one of the farms. This was music to my ears.

Chapter 13

Customs and Exercise

The village and its folk had many customs and beliefs and regular habits, such as the in thing for the men when their week's work was done was to visit the market town of Diss, some five miles away, on a Saturday night. They would walk by the footpaths across the fields and meadows and would often bring home the meat, which was as much as they could carry for five shillings (25p). This may appear cheap, but remember it was a quarter of a week's wages – how many today would spend a quarter of their wages on meat? Shops would be open until 9 or 10 p.m. Picture the poor barber's assistants finding their shops full at closing time. On the Market Place the Salvation Army played. Someone preached and some went round with collecting boxes at the same time. There would be acts of some sort, such as a man being put into a straightjacket, then chained, then put in a sack which was securely tied, only to escape to the applause of the large crowd which would gather and throw pennies onto a tarpaulin. Sometimes a bear would perform. This was all part of country life. The men would have a pint, light their pipes and return home across the footpaths, perhaps pouncing on some unsuspecting rabbit hiding in the grass, cracking its neck. 'They will be an extra dinner this week,' they would think, as they puffed away at their shag tobacco.

The women also walked into Diss now and again. I remember being taken, as a very small boy, by mother across the fields to the town. The first time was certainly an experience for me, having up until then seen nothing but the village where we lived, with no shops and suddenly being confronted with such an array of shops. To see so many goods all at once and in such variety was unbelievable. The shops had as many things on the pavement as inside, or so it appeared to me. The ironmongers with all their different tools on display; the basket maker with his handiwork hanging outside his shop – bushell skeps, linen baskets etc. I had never seen such a variety of baskets before. Outside a big grocer's shop were stacks of huge round cheeses, sacks of nuts, sides of bacon, all in the street. When I asked my mother what the big round things were, she told me 'Cheese, that's how it comes to the shopkeeper.' A few minutes later, a dog came along and cocked its leg up. I told my mother 'That dog has just peed on the cheese,' to which she replied 'That's all right, it's got a thick rind, it won't do any harm!'

When we started our journey back, I walked slap bang into an iron post on the edge of the pavement on which the warning words DO NOT SPIT were displayed. I found out later these were positioned all over Diss at strategic points and as time went by I realized why these signs were put up. Most of the men in the country chewed tobacco, which caused them to spit an awful lot. Often, when they were killing time on the farm or in the village, they would make a mark on the ground, or place a tin or stone for a target, and stand back and see who could hit the target by spitting. Not a very nice thought, but one of the many simple things men would get up to in those days. That's the reason the notices were put up. In the public houses, however, the landlords had to put up with it to sell their beer. Perhaps several men would be chewing and spitting, so 'spittoons' were provided. The floors were covered in sawdust to soak up all the beer which was spilled. There was plenty of spillage as all the beer had to be carried up from the cellars, pint by pint, and this became increasingly difficult as the Landlord would often become as unsteady as his customers. In those days beer was only 4d a pint (less than 2p) and they used to say if you had a 'snack lifter 2d' (meaning enough to open the door) you could come out drunk. There were plenty of pubs as the men had nothing else to do with their spare time in the dark winter evenings. Homes were so full of children – some families had 12 or more and the men were glad to get out of the way and their poor overworked wives were glad to see the back of them so they could get on with their never-ending chores, including making and altering clothes for their many children and the older girls had to do their fair share of the work.

There were no bathrooms; everyone had their turn to bath in the kitchen in a big galvanised bath which was placed in front of the fire. Water, which came from the well, would be heated in the copper built into the wall and would be transferred by jug to the bath. Several had to bath in the same water and this only took place once a week.

The day for washing the clothes was always Monday. All the washing had to be put through a large mangle before being hung out on the line if it was fine. If it was wet, all the clothes would be hung about the rooms to dry and air. This would sometimes take days and the fathers would curse when they came home, especially if they got a wet article of clothing in their faces. I was in a house on one such occasion when the father came home after a hard day's work in not too good a temper and he walked into his wife's bloomers which were large and he shouted 'Can't you hang your apple gatherers somewhere else?' They called that particular item of clothing apple gatherers, I still don't know why!!

One woman in the village was known as 'the twice sixteen woman' as she had sixteen children; as one died she had another. It was hard to bring up such large families, especially from the hygiene point of view. There were no drains so all the dirty water had to be thrown out each time the bowl was used. This would make a slimy mess just outside the back door. You always had to look out in case someone was coming round the corner of the house, and on more than one occasion my mother had to clean someone up after throwing a bowl of water over them. This was always accepted as part of living in the country and most would whistle or cough to let you know they were coming. There were no flush toilets or even pails then and the w.c. was always as far away from the house as possible, at the bottom of the garden. They were known as 'Bumbies' and were a masterpiece of ingenuity, being constructed over a large pit which would take a year to fill. With such large families, one seat was not enough so there were always two, one for the adult and one for the child. I have known of some with three and even one with four seats all side by side. With such large families, seldom did you have the toilet to yourself but nobody seemed to mind sharing in those days – men, women and children all together. These toilets would often be back to back with your next door neighbour and very often a running conversation would take place between the men. To reach this important room at night was a nightmare experience as there were no lights, only the lantern or candle. When you had to use a candle it was often blown out before you could complete the long journey from the house so you nearly always had someone to accompany you as the garden was a spooky place, with the rats scurrying and the leaves rustling. It was much worse if you had to come downstairs in the middle of the night and open the door with the wind howling, especially if there was a dead person in a nearby house. We children had such vivid imaginations and always feared the worst. I am including these experiences in great detail as I feel that in the years to come few people will believe these things I have described to be true, but indeed they are. To conclude my story concerning the little room, we children were constantly kept busy cutting newspaper into squares, through which a hole was made and string put through, and the finished bundle hung within easy reach of all the seats. Toilet paper had not then been invented!

Chapter 14

More Customs

Every home was indebted to the Squire and his family at some time or another. At Christmas time there would be gifts for the people of the Parish. Sir Edward gave every house a seven or eight pound joint of beef, which was a great treat as we chiefly had pork all year as beef was too expensive. He would also give each house a brace of rabbits, while the Head Person received a brace of pheasants; the women were given a large packet of tea and some of the poorest families received clothes which had been made by the servants at the Hall. These families had ten, twelve or more children and there was no family allowance. Their children with clothes of many patches looked poor and they were poor. Also, when anyone was ill, there would be large jugs full of soup and beef tea sent from the Hall to help their recovery.

20 December was the birthday of the Squire's daughter, Miss Molly. Each year the whole school would be invited to the Hall to receive a present from her. This was another high day in our lives and Sunday suits would be worn by the boys and the girls would wear their best dresses. We had to march to the Hall at exactly 12 noon, through the half mile of tree-lined avenue known as The Drive, which was like walking through the Holy of Holies to us as no-one was allowed to use the drive except the people who lived at the Hall. So we felt very proud and privileged as we marched along. When we reached the Hall we were met by the Squire's daughter outside the Conservatory and she would then call each of us to receive our presents which were always a very good book each and some fruit and buns. We each had to say 'Thank you Miss Molly, Happy Birthday,' then the boys would salute and the girls would curtsey (we had practised this many times). We then took our leave, the oldest boy or girl leading the way through a passage in which we would stop for a moment

and all shout 'Three cheers – hip hip hooray, hip hip hooray, hip hip hooray.' It sounded very loud in that passage! We would then return to school and resume our lessons for the day.

Everyone kept chickens and rabbits and some kept pigs, too, so we children were always doing something as at a very early age we were made to help look after the animals, which we thought of as pets. The women folk would always talk to the chickens to 'make them lay better'. One day I was talking to them in the same way as I had heard my mother. The hens all stood looking at me through the netting, expecting me to throw something for them to eat, when I decided I wanted to have a pee. I put my willie through the netting and a hen made a great peck at it. I screamed and mother came running to me. When I told her what had happened, she nearly passed out with laughing, so did the men when they heard. Once more I became the subject of humorous remarks such as 'Have you fed the chickens lately?'

Chapter 15

Steam Horses

One day my father said to Mother 'I hear the fair is at the King's Head at Dickleburgh. I think I will go there and take the boy to see the steam horses.'

'Steam horses?' I said but Father just said 'You will see.' I will never forget that first sight of the steam-driven roundabout, with all the horses going up and down and the music playing seemingly in time with the movement of the horses. The love of that machine was born in me at that moment and has remained with me ever since. Father took me for a ride and sat with me on the inside horse, which was safer. When I went home that night I felt as if I was walking on air, such was my joy at the experience I had just had. I could not stop talking about it. I told the children at school the next day and they were all envious and said they would see if their parents would take them and if they could afford the 1d to go on the ride.

As the years went by many events took place which I remember vividly. There was the occasion when the main road was having a face-lift with the stones I mentioned earlier. This was always a diversion from the usual village routine and we got to know the steam-roller driver over the years. The last time he visited our stretch of road, we sat and talked to him during his dinner (lunch) hour outside his caravan. One day he said to us 'I shall have a young chap with me next week learning this job. You will like him once you get to know him.' Sure enough, the next week there was another man with our usual engine driver. We saw them as they were about to have their dinner. We were told the new man was called George. As he got his frail basket out (all workers had frail baskets in those days), out of the top was sticking a long thing wrapped in a cloth. Our engine driver asked 'Whatever have you got there, all wrapped up?' George replied 'I only got married the other week and my wife don't know much about cooking. I said I liked rhubarb and she didn't know she had to cut it up, so she wrapped some dough round it and cooked it. I daren't say anything in case I upset her.'

We never saw George again and shortly afterwards we heard the road was to be tarred. A few years later it was and it was then that the spinning top became all the rage. Every boy in every school owned a top which he could spin with ease on the newly tarred roads. A hob nail would be knocked into the top of the wooden top to make it spin faster. Many and varied were the makes which came onto the market: the Flying Dutchman was the best but only the better-off boys could afford this one as it cost 6d. Most of us had plain ones which cost 1d or 2d each.

It was at this time that an astute businessman saw how these black tarred roads could be turned into something to his advantage. On the roads he had painted in large white letters 'Brames for wireless'. Now horses at that time trotting with their carts and carriages had only just got used to hearing their feet rattle on the new hard roads and suddenly they were confronted with these great white letters painted at quarter mile intervals from Stonham to Long Stratton. They slid to a stop, then made an almighty jump to clear the letters, nearly throwing the people out of the carts. So the white letters had to go and so were covered by a coating of black paint to match the tar.

In 1926 the same businessman created great interest when he introduced the first electric gramophone to the area. Geofrey Brame gave a public demonstration at Diss Corn Hall of this wonderful invention.

Chapter 16

The Wind Doth Blow

It was during my schooldays that most things seemed to happen. To a very young boy, the first time anything happens is always the best and although the same things happen many times in your life there is nothing like the first. I have mentioned the steam horses, the steam plough and new farm machinery and all these happenings are still fresh in my memory because they meant so much.

The next big event was the coming of the Wild Beast Show 'Bostock and Womwells' to Diss. We were rather frightened when we heard these wild animals would be coming through our village on their way from Norwich to Diss. I think they stopped at Long Stratton on the way to give the elephants a rest because they walked all the way. The day they were due to come past our teacher let us go into the playground so we could see. There was one steam engine which seemed to be pulling about ten cages from which came the grunts and growls of the occupants, which we could not see. Then came about twenty horses pulling the remainder of the cages and the accommodation vans and vans of fodder. The elephants brought up the rear, stopping at certain houses which had given them an apple or a bun in previous years – the elephants always seemed to remember. We were very excited and could hardly wait for Father to take us. We had to start early because it was a five mile walk across the footpaths. When we got there, what a sight! All the cages were placed in an oblong shape about 60 yards long and 40 yards wide, all covered with a huge tarpaulin. The engine was quietly puffing away providing the light for two or three great bulbs. Outside the entrance was a stall which sold buns, bananas, apples and nuts for the public to feed to the two elephants, which were standing by the entrance swaying backwards and forwards, swinging their trunks in anticipation of the treat to come. They were well trained in

The children and teachers of Thelveton School, 1925. L to R: Front row – Jonnie Moore; Marjorie Lawrence; Sybil Lawrence; Peter Potter. 1st row – Eric Cox; William Moore; Bertie Saunders; Frank Coulson; Author; Phyllis Moore; Marjorie Neal. 2nd row – Herbert Mullenger; Brenda Lawrence; Ivy Cox; Freda Kerry; Violet Lawrence; Kathleen Emptage. 3rd row – Vera Mullenger; Ruby Foreman; Ruby Hammond; Ethel Moss; Gladys Moore. Teachers: Left: Miss Grace Cook (Infant teacher). Right: Mrs. Smith (Head Teacher).

this, as was the boss of the show, who arranged the food so temptingly for the crowd to buy. Once we were inside there was another never to be forgotten sight. To we country folk it was amazing to see these great creatures padding up and down their cages and to hear their deep-throated growls. We had never seen any such animals before and to be truthful we were rather frightened. During the evening a boxing match was staged between two kangaroos – they looked very real to me, I suppose that's how they were supposed to act. When the performance was over, we drifted towards the exit and here the shrewdness of the owners was more in evidence as, while we were watching the show, the stall of buns had been craftily brought inside the tent, together with the elephants, to encourage us to feed them once more.

While on the subject of my very first visit to the Wild Beast Show, I will relate an amusing story which actually happened many years later. The same show was again visiting Diss and it was patronised by many hundreds of people from the surrounding villages who mostly cycled there so it was usual to see hundreds of bicycles lining the hedge of Annesse's Meadow where the Show and Fairs were held. Two such men cycled from a nearby village one night and one said to the other 'We shall never get in, look at all the people.' His friend replied 'Have your money ready and keep close to me.' They both went to the outside of the queue near the paybox and after a few minutes waiting, the people close to the front of the queue started to cough and gasp as if they were holding their breath (which they were). Suddenly a gap appeared close to Charlie and his friend, who said 'Now's our chance, get in there quick' so they found themselves in front of everyone and were soon inside enjoying the show. Charlie's friend boasted 'There you are, I knew I could shift them, I had fried onions for my tea!' to which Charlie replied 'You nearly shifted me, too!'

The country folk were self-supporting in many ways; as everyone kept chickens there was a plentiful supply of eggs. Any surplus eggs would be collected each week by an Egg Collector. He would come to the village with his horse and trap and the eggs he collected were sent to London, chiefly for the hotel trade. One week on visiting Charlie (the one I mentioned before) he remarked 'It's a pity your hens don't lay brown eggs.' Charlie thought 'If it's brown eggs he wants, brown eggs he will get.' So without more ado, he went to his shed and put some sawdust on the floor and then sprinkled it all over with strong coffee, turning the sawdust brown. As the hens produced their eggs, he rolled them about in the sawdust until every egg was a lovely golden brown colour. When the collector came, he said 'Ahh! you've got some brown eggs for me, I will give you ld more a score for them, like I promised.' (Eggs were sold by the score in those days, rather than by the dozen). Country folk were not all simple!

My aunt lived in a thatched cottage at Rushall where the thatch was within reaching distance of the ground and after dark every so often she would reach her hands under the thatch and bring out a sparrow which was sleeping; then if it was thin she would put it back for another time but when she had found about a dozen fat ones she would wring their necks, pluck them and have sparrow pie next day for dinner. She used to say 'I only cook the breasts - they are what you call good'.

One way the men had a little luxury food was when they decided to have fish to eat for a change. Sea fish were hard to come by and were too dear anyway. So what they did was get a large stone bottle and put a handful of carbide inside and put the cork back having placed a quill (large feather) through the cork. The cork would be wired tight and the whole thing fixed to a long piece of rope at the end of which was attached a very heavy iron hurdle wheel or something heavy enough to sink the bottle when they reached the river. They would put some of these bottles in sacks and under cover of darkness would walk a couple of miles until they reached the river. They knew where all the best holes were for the fish and would throw the bottles into the water and wait. As the water trickled through the quill in the cork and reached the carbide inside, a terrific build-up of gas occurred until the bottle exploded with the result that several fish were stunned and floated to the surface where the men, with their long sticks, would be waiting to guide them to the side where they would be quickly snatched out of the water and be put in the waiting sacks. Sometimes they would get as many as twenty good-sized fish and, if they were lucky, an occasional large pike would be included.

Yes, there were many and varied ways of obtaining a little extra for the table, mostly known only to the poachers, who were the specialists at their own game and had special dogs, too. There was one well-known poacher who the keepers and the police were most anxious to catch in the act. Try as they might, they could not catch him until one day the keeper came across him with his dog near some woods. The keeper confronted the poacher: 'Right, I've got you now, with your dog, on private land, after some game.' The poacher replied 'That old dog won't catch anything. He don't know anything about chasing game.' By this time the keeper had been joined by the policeman, who said 'We will soon see about that.' The poacher retorted 'All right, if you can get that old dog to run after anything I'll be surprised.' The keeper then commanded the dog 'Go on boy, hunt,' but the dog did not move. Then he said 'Rabbits!' – most dogs will respond to this but he still sat still. Then the policeman joined in, saying to the dog 'Come boy, let's go hunting pheasants.' Still the dog sat, not moving and by this time both policeman and keeper were very frustrated. After consulting one another, they decided to play their master card. With a great big 'We've-got-you-now' grin on their faces they said to the poacher 'Well, if he won't go for us, he will go for you. Go on, you send him hunting.'

The poacher shrugged: 'If you say so, but he won't go.' With that he shouted to the dog in a very commanding voice 'Go and hunt, fetch boy, go on, rabbits!' Still the dog sat there and the poacher said 'Now perhaps you will believe me, my old dog won't poach.' With that ringing in their ears the policeman and the keeper ordered the poacher back on the road and left with the parting shout 'We will get you soon.' The poacher did a sly grin and looked at his dog. That night several friends of the poacher had a little extra ready for dinner the next day. In fact, the dog was a very good poacher and could catch anything on four legs but the poacher had owned his dog from when he was a very small puppy and from his lonely cottage he trained it to his way of working. He would never let anyone near the dog until he was sure it would only obey the words he had taught it, which took over a year in training. His secret was that he had taught the dog 'backwards' as he would explain, which meant if he wanted the dog to hunt, he would say 'Stay'. If he wanted the dog to sit, he would command 'Hunt' or 'Go on, fetch'. The dog, as demonstrated earlier, was well trained, very well trained!

Coppers and ovens were built into the walls of the houses with a connecting chimney which was hard to sweep, so the only way to clean the soot from these complicated chimneys was to take some bricks out which was a lengthy job. These country folk soon thought of a better and quicker way than going to all that trouble. When they wanted to clean their chimneys, they would obtain two pennyworth of gunpowder from their local grocer (who stocked most things). The gunpowder was wrapped in very small packets, just enough to do the job intended. The packets would be placed in the back of the stove, then plenty of newspaper would be wedged in tight between the gunpowder and the front door of the stove. This paper would be lit and then the door hastily shut and wedged tight with heavy objects, mostly bricks. A wait of a few minutes and then 'woosh! bang!' the gunpowder would explode and all the soot would be blown out of the chimney, leaving it as clean as a whistle.

One day, the local grocer, Alfred, turned up at one of the cottages in his nice white apron as he regularly did. The lady of the house greeted him on the doorstep, saying 'Morning Alfred, could you help me out?' Alf was a very obliging chap and said 'I will if I can, what is it you want me to do?' The housewife said 'My old man has gone to work, he forgot to blow my chimney out and I can't get on with the washing until I can light the fire. That badly wants doing so do you know anything about using the gunpowder in these stoves? I got some here ready.' Alf admitted he had never done anything like this before but that he was willing to have a go. The woman said 'It won't take you long. I am afraid of the stuff or I would do it myself.' Alf took the gunpowder, placed it in the stove, put the paper in, lit it, shut the door and stood in the garden with the woman to watch the soot come out of the chimney. 'Bang' went the gunpowder but hardly any soot came out of the chimney. 'That's funny' said the housewife 'Perhaps it wasn't as bad as I thought.' But on re-entering the house, they both found out what had happened. Alf had forgotten to wedge the fire door, with the result that the explosion had sucked all the soot from the chimney and blown it into the room. When Alf related the tale he said 'You never saw such a mess, I had to spend nearly all day helping to clean it up as it was my fault. I looked like a sweep and all my other customers wondered why I was so late. The worst part was when I arrived back at the shop and had to explain to my boss. It will be a long time before I do that job again.'

Remember, we had very little to amuse us in those days, but many funny stories such as these were unfolding and we learned to laugh, often at ourselves, at some of the things which happened.

Chapter 17

Illness and The Cure

When an epidemic of any illness struck, it was considered very serious and, when the illness was influenza, as was often the case, the patient was confined to bed for two or three weeks, almost dying (and some did) during treatment. The nearest doctors were at Diss and to get a message to them meant walking five miles or sending a telegram via the postman, when he got back to Scole, which would take two or three hours. There were very few telephones anywhere and none in our village for many years. The doctor would arrive in his pony and trap and prescribe medicine which would have to be collected from the surgery that evening, meaning another walk to Diss. There were few pills or tablets, mostly medicine, which always seemed to taste horrible.

When scarlet fever hit the village, it was the most serious outbreak I can ever remember, the whole school was affected. Some were minor cases but some were serious and this was the only time I knew the school to close. I was confined to my bedroom for six weeks and was told afterwards that I had been the most seriously ill of the children and very near death. By this time the doctor had purchased his first car so things were slowly moving towards better times. Mother nailed a blanket over my bedroom door and sprayed it with Jeyes Fluid through which, the Health Department believed, germs could not escape. When I was declared well enough to leave my bedroom, the Sanitary Inspector from the Council arrived to fumigate the room which involved sealing up the windows. All books in the house were brought into the room and stood edgeways on the floor with their leaves open, all comics and papers had to be burnt. He then placed fumigating candles on the floor, set them alight and hastily retreated outside the door, which he also firmly sealed. We were told not to enter for twelve hours. I was not allowed out for at least another week.

50

The restrictions were very stringent in my youth and medicine has come a long way since then.

When I was first confined indoors, there were bare trees, no flowers and everything was still showing the effects of winter's drab. No one can take away from me the feeling I experienced when taking those first steps into the outside world, to see the trees in full leaf, the apple trees in blossom, the sight and smell of the sheeps parsley, now in full splendour. Even the stinging nettles looked lovely, it was like being reborn. I sat in the wheelbarrow, which was my favourite place, and surveyed this miraculous world and was lost in wonder and amazement at all the beauty around me as though it had been placed there for my benefit. I was eleven years old, had just been very near death, and being country born and bred had a great feeling and respect for nature which is still with me. Two doctors had been to see me on a Sunday at the peak of my illness, which was most unusual and a sure sign that I was extremely ill indeed. When I returned to school, that even looked better, I discovered that it too, had been fumigated, as had all the schools which had been infected with the dreaded scarlet fever.

All children had to have their hair combed regularly and checked for nits and fleas. It was a very necessary chore which we hated particularly as most of us were clear of these pests, but it was no surprise to see fleas jump on the book in which you were writing: at school we took it all as a matter of course.

In the autumn we school children were expected to go acorning. When the acorns began to drop the farmers would provide the sacks and we would make a beeline for the best and largest acorn trees – there was a difference, some trees produced very small acorns while others bore extra large ones. Over the years we soon came to know where the best ones were and would try to get there first to fill our tins up quickly. When the sacks were full we put labels on stating who had filled them and the farmer's foreman would collect and weigh each sack at the farm. At the end of the week he would pay our parents five shillings per hundredweight. This money was used to buy us boots and clothes. Our parents would give us a little at Christmas which we spent at our nearest shop, over a mile away. It was a very small shop but it appeared to sell everything. I can remember the shopkeeper, who was very tall and had to stoop all the time as the ceiling was so low. Our special treat was liquorice bootlaces or broken biscuits which could be purchased by the pennyworth. To us it was a very interesting shop and full of surprises. I even purchased an air gun there in my later years at school for four and sixpence. Ammunition was also supplied. Several boys owned air guns and I can honestly say I cannot remember anyone ever getting injured by one of these dangerous guns. We would shoot dozens of sparrows which were a pest to the farmer, and rats which we would hit when they ventured out during the day to steal the chickens' food. Our fathers would say 'Well done boy, shoot plenty more.' The gamekeepers did not like us having these guns in case we shot a game bird but they need not have worried as we were too scared to shoot anything like that. We were as frightened as our parents when it came to anything which would incur the anger of the Squire, for fear of the consequences.

Our school years seemed long then but remembering all the games we enjoyed there seemed to be a season for every game. Top spinning, hoop bowling, rounders, tip cat, hop scotch, marbles and conkers, all seemed to have their own season and many other enjoyable pastimes were organized by the school. Our favourite was the paper chase. We would spend hours tearing paper into small pieces the night before. When collected together the next day, the teacher would provide two large haversacks into which she put all the paper, then the two fastest runners in the school would set off on a two or three mile run across the footpaths and meadows, dropping a trail of paper all the way. Many false trails were laid to check the hounds (we children who followed) - the hares were the two runners. What a lot of fun this caused, litter did not seem to matter.

Another pastime was collecting birds' eggs; this was encouraged by our elders as there were thousands of birds about, the great wide and tall hedges which abounded everywhere were teeming with wildlife. There were hundreds of birds' nests of all descriptions and although we took the eggs we would never completely rob a nest. As we loved our birds it was an unwritten law never to empty a nest. To get a moorhen's egg, we would get a long stick to which we tied a spoon, we could then reach out to the nest suspended on a branch way out over the water in the pond. We often took five or six eggs from a clutch of nine, as our mothers liked to make cakes using water hens' eggs. Sometimes we were lucky on these expeditions and would come across wild ducks' eggs lying on the bottom of the ponds, these would be a special treat for our household when we got home.

I was at the age when I was supposed to do jobs on the farm on Saturdays. One job I liked doing, which was very dangerous although I did not think so at the time, was cake crushing. At the Manor Farm was a mill which was three floors high – the bottom floor consisted of the oat crusher, the second floor held the corn grinder, and the top floor was where all the corn was stored after having been pulled up through a series of trap doors which had a flap on each to prevent the corn sacks returning down. The corn would be shovelled down the shutes to the grinder or crusher and all this was driven by the portable steam engine via a belt. From the driving shaft on the second floor a belt passed through the wall to where the cake crusher was placed in a room on its own, this was known as the cowman's room. This was where all the cake and food for the cows was stored. The linseed cake came in big slabs, each weighing three stone, which had to be placed in the feed rollers of the crusher to be drawn out of sight into the machine which would crush the cake to bite-size pieces. This was a very dangerous job for a man, let alone a boy, with the belt flying round, and the danger of having one's arm being pulled into the machine, yet I was given this job when I was just twelve years old with the remark from the foreman 'You are just old enough, I left school at nine. Just mind what you're doing, that's all.' I ground a good half ton some days.

Another Saturday I was given a job of walking over the meadow with a reap hook, cutting down thistles: I hated this job. My love was the horses and the workers were muck-carting that day. I had heard it said that someone was needed to drive the full tumbril to the fields and bring the empty one back. So I threw my reap hook into the pond, telling the men at the farm it had flown out of my hand, so could I drive the horse in the tumbril? Which I did. When the foreman saw what I was doing, he gave me a great dressing down, telling me in no uncertain terms that when he set the men to work that was where he expected them to stay, until he said they could go.

One day my father was using the self-binder in the twelve acres cutting oats and the local warrener was told not to shoot in that field as my father had a young horse he was trying out which was rather nervous. The very thing he was told not to do, he did, with the result that the horses took off, taking the binder with them. My father held on for a time but eventually fell off backwards, nearly breaking his back on the hard ground. The horses carried on at breakneck speed with the binder sails flying round kicking up a terrible clatter. The horses jumped the hedge and ditch, breaking the main pole (hostelry) completely off, leaving the binder across the ditch. The horses carried on down the lane until they had exhausted themselves and came to a standstill. In the meantime my father was getting up and he staggered to the side of the field and said 'I shall be all right I expect, I might have broken my neck, bloody fool shooting near the horses like that. You had better tell the foreman, boy, he is in the long

Ten Acre New Field, you can get there quicker than us.' Off I ran across the fields to tell the foreman. On my arrival he asked why I was running and when I explained the first thing he said was 'Is the binder broken?' Not 'Is your father all right' which shows how much the men came second to the machines. They cost money to repair – men nothing, and plenty of them about!!

Chapter 18

Scouting Days

When I was considered old enough to join the Scouts, the first thing I had to do was put on my best suit and go to the Hall to have tea with the Scout Mistress. I was ushered into the dining room and then waited on at table by the Butler. This was a great day for we who were joining the Troop. After tea, we were measured for our Scout uniforms, a proud moment this. We were then told what the Scout Troop was all about and what we were each supposed to do once we had become Scouts. A good deed every day was expected of us. A room was given for our use at the Hall and the Scouts' night was always an occasion we looked forward to. Many games and competitions were arranged for our benefit and we had a trek cart which was used for all sorts of activities such as taking gifts from the Squire to the villagers and logs of wood to the elderly at Christmas time. We often had to pull the cart through very deep snow to reach our destinations. It was very rewarding, though, to see the looks of gratitude on the people's faces as they received their gifts. Every winter, when the Moor at Dickleburgh was frozen, we were taken by the Assistant Scout Master, Reg Warnes, to learn the art of skating; skates were provided by the Hall. In the summer we were taught how to swim when taken for weekend trips to the river. We had a lot to be thankful for from the teaching we received in the Scouts.

After each meeting we had to stand to attention while the Scout Mistress read the evening prayers to us; this was always a solemn occasion. We dare not misbehave during prayers. One night, when prayers were being said and we were all standing with our heads down, one of the boys broke wind – not once or twice, but several times in quick succession. There was an awesome silence. Then first one boy started to titter with laughter, then another and another. The Scout Mistress blushed and hastily concluded the evening's proceedings and beat a hasty retreat back through the door into the safety of the Hall, leaving the poor boy in question to hang his head down even lower than it was before. The Assistant Scout Master, who was an ex-navy man and understood these things, joined the boys in the laughter that followed. We never knew whether the Scout Mistress laughed in private!

Chapter 19

We Journey Forth

It was a rare treat to be taken to Great Yarmouth once a year on our choir outing. We would be picked up by wagonette and taken four miles to Pulham where we boarded a wonderful steam train; this was on the branch line from Tivetshall, now sadly gone for ever. What a wonderful sight to see the magnificent steam engine (man's most inventive gift) – we never thought these would be made redundant or scrapped. The train was all part of our lives, everything went by train, there was the Milk Train, the Coal Train, the Mail Train and the General Goods Train which carried everything from cattle to oil. Once in a while it would set a corn field or the embankment alight when the fireman threw out the spent ashes but we loved it all the same. People would set their watches by it and the men working in the fields would wave to it and sometimes the engine driver would wave back. Cattle would look up, then carry on grazing. Once in a while the menfolk would go by train to see their favourite football team and would gather at the end of the platform to gaze lovingly at the engine. Small boys would join in to gaze as it stood there with its great belly throbbing, steam trickling from an outlet and just a little smoke rolling from its funnel. The engine stood proudly displaying its power. Sadly nothing remains the same for ever, no one at that time told us that this magnificent machine would be replaced by a stinking yellow monster called a diesel train. We were not consulted and even if we had been it would have made no difference, replaced it was and the branch line was closed.

We lived in times of change in the early nineteen twenties and the first such change was the 'charabanc' which was amazing to all who saw it for the first time and was likened to a wagon without horses. It had solid tyres and could carry twenty people and when it rained a large hood would be

A Charabanc.

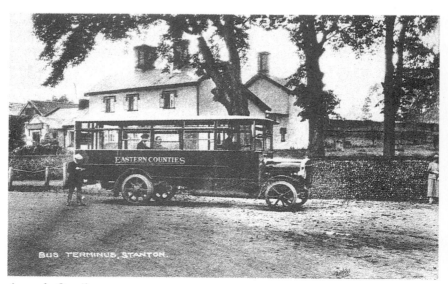

An early Omnibus.

pulled over the top. It was only allowed to travel at twelve miles an hour. One of these contraptions was bought by Mr Cook of the Ship Inn, Diss, and he ran a service to Norwich which took two hours. For a long while people were afraid to get on board this new-fangled carriage. It was not long before Mr Froud of Diss followed suit. His bus was named 'Nancy' and mystery trips were arranged for summer Sunday evenings, always finishing at a pub. The Eastern Bus Company (as they were called) were soon on the bandwagon but went one better and invented the double-decker which had an open top like the Charabancs but had no cover if it rained so everyone crowded down below. This company decided to run services from Ipswich to Norwich but before they could start the trees which abounded along the main road had to be cut back so that people who were travelling on the upper deck did not get plucked from their seats by the low, overhanging branches. To do this, they sent a bus with two men on the top deck armed with saws and long-handled pruners, and they cut off all they could reach until they had filled the upper deck with branches. The bus then disposed of the wood in a field and returned to carry on the operation. This took several weeks, watched by the horrified locals who hated to see their beloved trees being treated in such a way. At this time they did not know what was happening and when told there were going to be buses running a regular service along the road, they were alarmed and asked 'What about the horses and cows? Shall we be able to come along here when the bus comes?' One said 'We shall have to hear what the Squire says about this, he won't like it.' As it happened, he did not like it, or the infernal combustion engine, or even the roads being tarred, as this did away with grit for the birds and the game. So with the coming of the charabanc a new era had begun. People could now be picked up near their doors and not have to walk across the footpaths to the station to go to places like Norwich or Ipswich or Great Yarmouth. All the passengers had to get out and walk over Haddiscoe wooden swing bridge on the way to the coast, and then climb aboard again on the far side of the river, as it was considered the weight of a bus and its passengers would be too much as wooden bridges were not built for contraptions like that, so they said. When the first double-deckers started the service runs, almost everyone gathered by their garden gates to watch in awe as these brightly coloured, noisy buses came rattling along. Nothing like this had ever been seen before, and there were people waving from both decks as they went past. The top decks were fitted with wooden seats and the passengers would hold on for grim death at the height and speed they were travelling – twelve miles an hour on solid tyres!

It soon became obvious we had to accept these changes to our lives. This was just the beginning and there would be many more as our learned friend on the farm repeatedly said 'I told you so'.

The next change was a surprise. We heard all the cows were to be registered with the Ministry as they wanted to find a cure for tuberculosis. They wanted to test for TB in the milk and to do that every cow had to be tested, registered and numbered. All the cows were examined one by one and the older cowman got very frustrated ('het up' as they say). When asked by the Ministry man if a particular cow had been done yet, he replied 'I don't know, there are too many bloody black ones, go in the yard yourself, I have had enough of this.' With that he left the poor man with his papers and cleared off. This illustrates how the ring of change was accepted with great reluctance in some cases!

Chapter 20

The Age of the Bike

Bicycles were fairly common to the adults but we children were told we would have to wait until we went to work and earned enough to buy one. To our delight, a new family moved into our village and they owned a child's cycle. We were invited by the parents to learn to ride and so it came about every child in the school learned to ride on that one bicycle. Many years later my mother bought me my first bike when I reached the age of thirteen. This was from a five pounds legacy she had received from her service days and I was told it represented a whole year's wages in her time as a cook in service. She was paid five pounds and had a free uniform once a year, and lived in of course!

Like so many at the time, I found my new freedom a luxury I had never dreamed of. Cycling to the next village instead of walking gave me a feeling of importance. I was most anxious to please by volunteering to go on errands just to have the excuse to ride, while most of the other children had older cycles I had a brand new one, thanks to my mother's legacy, and I was proud of its gleaming paint and shining wheels and I was forever polishing it. For once I felt very rich, in those days of poverty, this was another move forward in our age of discovery.

Soon there were almost as many cycles as people and it became the chief method of travel around the villages. The menfolk found them to be the best thing invented so far, as now instead of the long walk to their favourite pub, they got there in no time at all, which made it possible for them to arrange quoit matches (their favourite game) during the summer with other distant pubs. Life was definitely more interesting for them. It was common to see as many as forty or fifty cycles outside a pub on important match days. Tools of their trade would be carried on the cross-bar. Shopkeepers had special cycles for their deliveries; even the ladies had special guards for their dresses on their tall upright cycles. Yes, the bicycle was very popular. Oil lamps were the only form of headlamp at the very beginning but, like everything else, this dim and very smelly item had to go and was replaced by the wonderful carbide lamp, which gave out a remarkably good light and manufacturers would compete with one another as to who could produce the best lamp. The young chaps of that era used to see who had the lamp which gave the best light; many shapes and sizes were produced ranging in price from four and sixpence (about 22p) up to twelve and sixpence (about 62p) for 'the best lamp in the world' or so it was called. It was made by Lucas and proud was the owner of one of them. It was thought he must be very rich to be able to afford such an expensive light – almost a week's wages to some. Lamps were fitted with an extension tap where a length of rubber tube would be attached to a rear light – very posh, we thought. Cycles were not used by farm workers to get to work because again they were worried that the farmer would think they were overpaid. No, it was better to walk they thought and would often still walk several miles to work.

Then cars began to appear in increasing numbers, instead of the odd one and the weekly skin lorry which had solid tyres and was chain driven. It passed our school, creating a terrible stench from the skins of the animals laying flat on the open back; the skins were collected from the butchers in the area. Our lives were changing as other solid tyre lorries and vans began to appear. 'Brooke Bond' vans began passing regularly and what with the occasional charabanc and double-decker, it was getting quite busy and almost too much for the quiet country folk to take in. I remember the young men of the village saying 'I counted twelve vehicles going through here today, whatever are we coming to?' Such was the novelty to us children, we used to lay on the road with our ears to the ground so we could hear if something was coming from a long way away – there was plenty of time for this between motors.

Chapter 21

More Customs and Habits

Wells were the main source of drinking water. One would be situated within walking distance of cottages, all of which depended on the one well for all their daily needs. During the summer an increased volume of water was needed for the large amount of washing due to the very large families. Often water had to be carried almost a quarter of a mile to the isolated cottages. The men would use a yoke, a piece of wood shaped to their shoulders, with two chains hanging to which two pails would be hooked. This made carrying easier but it would still be hard work when making two or three journeys before going to work, especially if the weather was rough.

Often a pail would come unhooked from the chains used in the well and another pail would have to be purchased. When several pails were lost, the men would get together and organise a 'pail hunt' as they called it. They would use a set of creepers or grapplers attached to a long plough line and one man would lean over the well and try to hook the lost pails. They were pulled to the top of the well, often full of water or silt, making this a very dangerous job for the man doing the job. The other men hung on to him to prevent him from pitching head first down the well. If they pulled up a pail belonging to someone they did not like, they would say 'Bugger him, let him get his own pail out,' and they would throw the pail back down the well.

In the middle of the nineteen twenties, British Summer Time, altering the clocks, was introduced. For the first time clocks all had to be put forward by one hour. One man in the village refused to accept this 'Meddling about with God's time'. The first day it came into force, he walked to the next village, which was a mile away, arriving at his favourite pub at exactly half past nine at night, only to find it closed. He banged on the door but was told the pub was closed and had been for half an hour as it was now half past ten because new time had started. 'New time,' he shouted. 'There's no such thing; God's time is God's time and you can't alter that.' He fumed and swore all the way home, looking at his watch all the way; he never did alter that.

The great drought was in 1921: the year when all the ponds went dry with the exception of one known as 'The Smugglers' which was very deep. Half of it did dry up, but the half which still held water had to supply the village with water for the cattle, the water being transported in water carts. Ponds were a must and because horses could not work without water, they always had a special pond near their stables known as 'The Horses' Pond'. That year, even they dried out and the men set to work cleaning them out which entailed a lot of hard work. All the mud of years was dug out by hand and was five feet deep in places. It was pulled clear by two horses dragging a tumbril and the contents were then carted to surrounding fields and spread by hand with wooden shovels. There was so much goodness in this mud that the resulting crop of Clog Wheat grown on these fields reached the height of six feet and proved almost too long for the self-binder to handle. The shoves were so heavy with grain that it took a superhuman effort to lift each one onto wagons at harvest time. Twenty-two combs of wheat were recorded per acre: a record.

There were some very strong men about who were able to deal with this problem, as I found out to my surprise. One day I was rather cheeky to one of these men until he could bear my cheek no longer. He calmly grabbed me by the scruff of my neck with one hand and the backside of my trousers with the other and with one almighty swing he threw me on top of the load of corn which was a good eight feet high. I just managed to hold on to prevent myself from going over the top. I was ten years old at the time and weighed about five stones so this was no mean effort. This incident proves how strong the men were and taught me a lesson I never forgot. I was never cheeky to anyone again.

All sorts of unusual things were part of the farm life, which we took in our stride and came to accept, like watching the cowman milk. There was very little hygiene – seldom were cows' udders washed, it was not considered necessary, and no one ever came to any harm from the milk and the butter was delicious. One superstition was that the bladder or afterbirth from a cow which had just calved had to be hung on a hawthorn hedge to ward off the danger of an abortion. As a result, all the hedges in the vicinity of the farmyard were covered with these reminders of recent births.

Animal reproduction became quite natural to us children. At first sight of animals mating we were told not to look but after a time we got used to it and called them the 'Piggy-Back Animals'. Of all the births we witnessed, the small chicken coming from an egg was the favourite sight. Chickens were allowed to roam free in the farmyards and eggs were to be found anywhere. Cockerels roamed with the hens, so any eggs laid were fertile and the hen concerned would sit on the clutch of eggs wherever they were and would often return with ten or twelve chickens, so the eggs were never lost. Some farmers were so concerned about their hens laying in the neighbouring fields that they would give a 'Trailing Gotch' (a gallon of beer) to the person who found a nest of eggs when mowing round the field at harvest time. Sometimes more than one hen would lay in the same nest with the result that there would be thirty or more eggs in the nest. One farmer who was known for his meanness was caught out by two crafty men who were mowing in the field next to his stackyard. One went into the farmer's chicken house and brought out about twelve or fourteen eggs in his cap, while the other made a small hole in the bottom of the hedge, then stamped the grass down to make a small track in the corn. They then trod a small patch through the corn and made a nest into which they placed the farmer's eggs. After a while the farmer appeared and one of the men shouted to him 'What about a trailing gotch?' The farmer denied that his hens ever strayed.

'Oh well,' said the man 'You won't want these eggs then.'

'What eggs?' asked the farmer and he jumped the ditch to where the men were working. They showed him the trail leading to his farm and the eggs, which he promptly gathered up, saying 'I had better get your gotch,' which he did, to the chuckles of the now happy men.

I remember too the sight of a tramp shuffling along with his tin tied to his waist. There were many more tramps in those days and they looked very frightening to us; even the womenfolk would bar their doors when one appeared at the gate. If anyone encouraged them by giving them food or water, they would leave a sign with stones near the gate for the next tramp to read, and the people whose gate the stones were placed near dare not move the stones for fear of a curse.

The same fear of disaster was again evident when a thunder storm was raging. All mirrors would be turned to the wall or covered up, knives would be put away out of sight and everyone had to get up at night in case the house was struck by lightning. Storms were frequent in July and August and were much worse than they are today. A storm would be brewing all day, with distant rumbles getting louder and louder, the sky would be black for several hours before the storm really broke. When it did, it was very frightening. Lightning could sometimes be heard to snap and the smell of sulphur was sometimes experienced. This would perhaps last all night and would be the talking point the next day, especially the rain, which accompanied the storm. Two inches would sometimes be recorded on the rain gauge at the Hall. All the ditches would be full of racing water and we would have great fun throwing sticks into the water and racing after them. Water like this is seldom seen today but was a common sight then.

Another custom was as the fields were cleared of corn, each field would have sticks from the surrounding hedges stuck at intervals all over the field. This would be a signal that the farmer had finished with it and it could now be gleaned. The women and children descended on these fields and would often finish up with several sacks of ears of corn, which was a great help to them for feeding their poultry. Some families even gleaned enough to be exchanged for flour by the local miller. I would often go with the others on these expeditions and sadly look up at the tall hedge near the gate at a few strands of golden straw which had been snatched from a passing load: the harvest was over and we must now prepare for winter.

Chapter 22

I Leave School

I reached the age when my wonderful days at school were nearing their end and I was beginning to prepare myself for the adventures ahead. According to what I heard from the knowledgeable ones, I would find a very different world out there from that which I had been used to. I listened to the advice I was given but I had a mind of my own and decided that farm work was not for me, much as I loved it. I wanted to be a part of this world which was changing so rapidly. I applied for a job as a lorry boy with the Shell Mex Petrol Company stationed at Diss and was accepted, much to the delight of myself and my parents. The villagers were

Diss oil salesman.

67

apprehensive, saying 'You won't like that, riding on a stinking oil lorry all day and humping cans of paraffin about.' I could see a future in oil and petrol and went to work with a will, cycling the five miles each day to join the lorry which was a five-ton Thornycroft on solid tyres. It was a wonderful experience for me, climbing aboard for the first time. There were no side windows in the cab and we used to nail a sack up to keep out the cold winds and the rain and snow. The maximum speed we were allowed to travel was twelve miles per hour and the engine was fitted with governors to prevent speeding. There were three lorries stationed at Diss: one was a 'Guy' driven by Mr H Rolfe, one was an 'Albion' driven by Mr A Wright, and the 'Thornycroft' I was on was driven by Mr George Elliot, who was a very kind and understanding man. I was only a small fourteen-year-old and could hardly lift the five-gallon cans of paraffin which we had to carry two at a time to the various grocers and oil men who delivered door to door, as oil was the main source of light and heat. For a few weeks my driver would not let me carry but carried the cans himself and left me to fill them from the great big tanker. I soon got stronger and it was not long before I could carry as well as George. I had not been at work for more than a week when I was invited to learn to drive this great monster. I was told the sooner I learned the better driver I would become, so I was first taught how to steer and would lean over and steer with George at the controls which were huge with a gate gear change and pedals as big as tea plates. I had to learn to double-declutch on hills, which was achieved with a great roar and clatter at first, but when mastered it could become a smooth and silent operation.

Chapter 23

Petrol Power

I soon got the hang of this job and the routine. Every morning we had to visit the depot at Diss Railway Station to load our lorry ready for the day's work. This meant pumping paraffin by hand from the tanker trucks which was a tedious job and it took quite a long time to fill the lorry from such a small pump. We then had to call at the main depot on Victoria Road in Diss to collect a few cans of petrol – about fifty each day. As there were only a few cars about, not many garages were equipped with a petrol pump at first but would tip the petrol in from the cans through a large funnel. Most of those early cars held a petrol can strapped on the running board – all cars had a running board at that time. Cars even had their batteries strapped on the running board. We supplied three brands of petrol: 'Shell Mex' at tenpence (4p) a gallon, 'Shell' at elevenpence halfpenny (5p) a gallon, and 'Aviation Spirit' at one shilling and three-pence (just over 6p) per gallon. The latter was chiefly used in a spare can on the running board, as the can looked so much better, being all golden in colour.

Petrol pumps were gradually installed at these early garages. Some of the garages were late bicycle shops and repair shops for the many motor cycles which had become popular. The early pumps were operated by hand and were wound first one way to release a half gallon of fuel, then wound back, then forward for the next half gallon. These were especially useful to fill motor cycle tanks which required a half gallon. It took several minutes to fill a car by this method as the cars were very thirsty on petrol but, as the petrol was cheap, those who could afford a car never minded. There was hardly one car in each parish in this year of 1928 – the year I started work. Even our Squire was a long time before he consented to turn away from his beloved horses and traps to the new combustion engine method of travel. Time finally overtook his way of life as he discovered. The day dawned when he arrived in London by train, as was usual every Monday and Wednesday morning, to find not his usual cabby there to take him to his place of business but a throbbing motor taxi. From that day he accepted he must go along or be left behind. When he arrived back at Diss station his own horse and carriage was waiting as usual and his driver was told reluctantly on the way home that the horses would have to go but the Squire promised he would keep them as long as he could.

'I shall have to get one of those confounded things,' he told his coachman. 'I thought I never would but my son tells me it's got to come, but I will prolong it as long as I can,' he said.

After a time the coachman moved on, a Rolls Royce was obtained and life at the Hall started a new era, more of which I will tell the reader later in these memories.

Scole Inn was the first private residence to have a petrol pump and quite a stir in the village it caused, too. There was much talking in the pubs about this strange thing which dished out petrol, with another smaller box-like contraption standing next to it with a pump attached, which provided oil for the motorist. The Scole Inn, in common with other large establishments, had its own electric light plant. When the petrol pump was installed, a wire was connected from the Inn to the bulb in the Shell Globe on the top of the pump. When the engine was started up, the globe would be lit, much to the wonderment of the country folk, who would gather round in large numbers when it was first used. People would even cycle or walk in from surrounding parishes just to see this wonderful thing – electric light. They had heard about it but never seen it and to them, and me, it was quite a miracle. I even heard some of the people clap and cheer when it began to light up. After a while, pumps began to spring up all over the place, it seemed anyone could have a pump if they wanted. As they all wanted to be in on the act, I expect there are many forgotten tanks in the back gardens of houses even now.

Although petrol sales were on the increase, paraffin was still the main source of income to the oil companies. There were many hawkers of paraffin in the district who travelled door to door and they sold many other different household requisites too, including scrubs, candles, floorcloths, bowls, lanterns, bootlaces, lamp glasses, blue bags and washing soda . One trader even sold sweets and 'rock balls' – he was known as Rock Balls. They all had horse-drawn vehicles and the horses would be allowed to feed along the grass verge while their owners were away at someone's house. Often the horses would pull the carts into the ditch. This, I discovered, was repeated in all the villages we visited with our lorry. We had a special discount for these hawkers if they ordered five hundred gallons or more. It was a halfpenny a gallon cheaper – down to sevenpence, which made a lot of difference. They would walk round to each house with a gallon or even a half gallon, so it can be imagined the walking they had to do to sell five hundred gallons. They would cover about an eight-mile radius going from door to door and sold this amount every week, whatever the weather.

The powers that be, sitting in their office in London, decided a charge would be made when deliveries were made outside a certain boundary, so they made a circle on the map to mark a ten-mile radius of Diss. It so happened that at Tivetshall two brothers farmed, one on either side of the boundary. So to get over paying the extra halfpenny a gallon, one would bring his cans and containers across the road to his brother's farm in a tumbril where we would fill them. As they both had the same name, we were well within the rules and on 100 gallons could save this farmer four shillings and twopence (21p) once a fortnight! Quite a lot of money in those days. On one of these farms there were some walnut trees and I was allowed to pick the nuts when we had delivered our order. I then sold them on our round at twenty for one penny. Sometimes I earned one shilling doing this and would feel quite rich as I only had two shillings pocket money each week. I remember saving my first three weeks' pocket money and buying my mother an aluminium teapot for six shillings, such was our love and respect for our parents, we felt as soon as we earned some money we wanted to repay them for all they had done for us.

By this time I was feeling the freedom that comes with growing up. I was very soon persuaded to visit the 'picture house' (cinema) by other boys of my age. This was a tin-roofed building at Diss and was very popular. There were only silent films then, with a piano playing in time to the scene which was being shown. The music was very much in keeping with the picture, the latest tunes being played for a comedy and very heavy music for dramas. We could only afford to attend the Saturday matinée which cost twopence to get in. The programme consisted of a five-minute comedy, followed by the news, then the serial, then a preview of forthcoming films, and finally the main picture. If there was a hailstorm during the show, the film was stopped because the terrible clatter on the tin roof would spoil the effect of the piano. After the storm the film would be restarted to much clapping and stamping of feet on the boarded floor – there were no carpets. To all the patrons this was an experience never to be forgotten. The pictures looked so real that most of us clapped the hero and booed the villain in the serial, which was shown twice a week. As we journeyed home after seeing a frightening film some of us were really scared after seeing things we had not previously known existed. The reader must realize there was no television or other diversion in those days and everything we saw or heard was magnified out of all proportion. The nearest I had been to seeing anything like this before was from a magic lantern my mother bought me for Christmas for three shillings and sixpence. I rigged up the lantern in a shed at home and had slide shows for the school children. Following this I worked the magic lantern for the Rector when he gave religious slide shows in our Working Men's Club.

The Working Men's Club, or Reading Room as it was known, was built in 1915 by Sir Edward with the express purpose of keeping the young men of the village on the straight and narrow. We were only just coming out of the Victorian age. Games were provided and concerts arranged. Once a year a dinner and smoking concert was held with all the food provided by the Squire, and what a meal it was! There would be huge joints of beef, large rabbit pies and vegetables, followed by massive apple pies and custard, all cooked at the Hall and all washed down with plenty of ale. A smoking concert followed with cigarettes provided from the same source. The concert artists were the workmen themselves. Sir Edward himself would be present and he loudly applauded the turns. I have seen the tears run down his face at the dry humour of our local grocer who was a master at telling a joke.

Yes, the villagers themselves provided their own entertainment in those days and some were the equal of the stars of today. Concert parties were formed where it was possible for all to get together and practice, not an easy task with very little transport available. There would be perhaps the piano player from one village, the comedian from another, and so on until the party was formed. The most successful party would be in great demand to perform, chiefly in schools, as there were very few village halls. The local carpenters would be called in to erect the stage and fix the curtains so they opened and closed properly. A farmer would lend a man and a horse and wagon to fetch the extra chairs needed from the next village and return them the next day. The school teacher would instruct the best writers in the school to write the programmes. If one of the popular parties were coming to our village, this would be talked about for weeks ahead, especially if a well-known local comedian was going to be present as in those days we lived for laughter – in every home there was laughter, despite the conditions the people were living in. Mothers had perhaps eight or nine children to feed and fathers coming in from work with four or five soaking wet sacks to dry in readiness for the next day. Sacks were worn as they could not afford coats and if it rained they carried on working if possible as if they stopped their wages were cut at the end of the week. The only coats available in the early twenties were the great coats worn during the First World War which the men were allowed to keep. I remember seeing them still being worn by some well into the nineteen thirties.

Chapter 24

Don't Eat The Bees

Soon after the Great War ended, people began to realize things were changing fast and many of the beliefs were beginning to fade with the new generation and new ideas that were constantly cropping up. Communications were slowly improving with some of the more adventurous young men straying further afield and returning with stories of the things they had heard. So conversation changed from the close village life to 'Have you heard . . .?' 'Fancy that!' and 'It can't be true'. 'I never heard such squit' (rubbish) said one villager when he was told bees were making wine in a village a few miles away. However, it was perfectly true. Although the bees were, in fact, pieces of a chemical which looked like small pieces of bread and they were introduced to the public by scientists. The 'bees' multiplied very rapidly when placed in a jar of water, and would work up and down in the jar constantly increasing in numbers all the time. They would be fed daily with sugar and the water would become wine which could be bottled and drunk almost at once. It had to be strained very, very carefully as the bees were supposed to be poisonous if eaten, so a fine piece of muslin was used. When completed and the wine extracted, a few 'bees' were saved to start the cycle again. The spare ones were given to anyone who wanted them. The village postman would know if anyone wanted them on his rounds and would let the person concerned know when anyone was straining the 'bees'. It soon became a common sight to see jam jars in almost everyone's window with the 'bees' at work. This practice lasted several years and stopped as suddenly as it had started, one knew not why, and I expect there are very few people alive today who can remember the 'Bees Wine' which was so strong and popular. I remember our 'bees' being thrown on the garden, I never knew the reason.

Chapter 25

People and Pubs

I had other things to think about, I was a teenager and my thoughts were on the more important things. I had a job to do and was so proud to bring my wages home to my parents – ten shillings for mother and two shillings for myself. As I travelled around the twelve-mile radius of Diss with our petrol lorry, I learned many things, chiefly the importance of people, the ones we met every week, the same day and at the same place, with the same cheery words. Some would be bubbling over to tell us something they would think would be news to us. Before we got out of the lorry sometimes a farmer or a shopkeeper would say 'Have you heard about old so and so?' News was slow to travel, so when a special item of interest was gleaned, the person concerned could not contain his excitement for long, he or she had to find someone to tell as quickly as possible. Such was the importance of anything new.

Much information came via pubs, of which there were many. I was soon to be introduced to this mine of information as I was allowed to stand just inside the passage of many a pub and enjoy some refreshment while my elders continued their business behind closed doors. The law was very strict concerning people under 18 drinking in the bar but it never seemed to matter if one stood in the passage – this never made sense to me. Many tales and true stories were told in pubs. Wagers were often taken over anything which resembled a chance. One farmer told his bar audience, who were boasting about the size of their turkeys, that no more than 5lb of meat could be got from a 25lb bird. They all thought he was wrong so it was arranged for a 25lb turkey to be killed and the Landlady to cook the bird and cut it up in front of everyone. The meat would then be weighed. The Landlady, who also held the stake money, duly obliged and try as they might by scraping every piece of meat from the bones, only 4½lb of meat could be found. The farmer smiled, then instructed the money to be spent on beer, which bought a considerable lot at fourpence a pint, with the result everyone returned home a little bit under the weather, but happy!

Another true story was concerning the farmer who had a very fierce dog which would allow no one anywhere near the farm when it was loose. So the farmer had to keep it chained to its kennel most of the time. The farmer himself was even wary of it, such was the character of this animal. There were few people who dare go to the farmer's door. Then one man in the public bar said to the farmer 'I can tame your dog, I am afraid of no dog, yours wouldn't frighten me.' The farmer said 'I will give you £5 if you can get near his kennel.' 'Done,' the man said. 'I will come with you now.' Away they went to the farm, which was only a short distance away, so several locals followed to witness the taming of the beast. Upon arrival at the farm they stood well back, while the farmer surveyed the scene from a distance with a wry smile on his face. The farmer and everyone had said the man was about to risk his life but he advanced to within six feet of the dog, which by now was nearly mad, frothing at the mouth and snarling. At this point the man stopped. Then he got on his hands and knees, took off his cap, put it in his mouth and waved it to and fro and up and down like an extended tongue. He made the most blood curdling noises and leapt up and down, making even worse noises. The dog stared at this apparition, not quite knowing what to do but suddenly, after about five minutes of this 'thing' getting nearer, the dog turned tail and vanished into its kennel, much to the astonishment of those who were watching, not least the farmer. The man had not finished yet. No sooner had the dog disappeared into the kennel than he followed close behind, leaving his backside wedged in the kennel entrance to prevent an escape and, while on all fours, he set about the dog. Such noise erupted from the kennel as had never been heard before. The unearthly noises from the man and the screams and howls of fear from the dog, who was at this time being bitten by this awful 'thing' in his home. The man did not let go, he bit the dog's ears until they bled, shouting all the time 'Now bite somebody you old **!! That'll learn you!' He then backed out of the kennel, leaving a very sorry looking dog curled up in the corner. The farmer, looking as white as a ghost, said 'I don't believe it. I never thought there was anyone who could get near him. Here's your £5, you've earned it.' The rest of the company present couldn't get back to the pub or home fast enough to tell what they had seen. Needless to say, the dog was never any more trouble.

Another true story concerning farm life was about a farmer living in the next village who paid £100 for a shire horse which was a lot of money. After a time, this horse had a sore foot which needed attention. As this was such a valuable animal, the farmer asked a friend what he should do to treat the horse's foot: there were no vets available, so most owners of sick animals had to treat them themselves. His friend advised him to put a bran poultice on it. The farmer thought that mixing some cow dung with it would give it better drawing power, so they got a sack and put a large quantity of cow dung mixed with bran into it; the mixture looked awful. They lifted the horse's foot up and lowered it into the sack and then tied the sack round the horse's leg to prevent it slipping off. The farmer, who had a long beard, fetched a kettle of boiling water and poured it over the sack to start the action of the poultice. The horse leapt up in the air and with an almighty kick the bran sack, with all its contents, smashed against the wall. The bag split and covered the farmer and his friend in cow dung and bran. The farmer looked a sorry spectacle with the contents of the sack dripping from his beard.

Cow dung was often used in the building of clay lump houses and buildings, and, mixed with lime, it was brushed on to provide a seal over the clay lump – it was called daub! Yes, many uses were found for lots of the things nature provided, like the use of large cobwebs to stop the flow of blood from a cut. It really worked – when anyone cut themselves in those days they would run into the nearest building and pull a handful of cobwebs from the walls or ceiling, there were always plenty, and sometimes they were full of dust, even coal dust, but it never seemed to bother the user, who would wash the blood off in the tank or pond and place the cobweb onto the open wound. He would then wind his spotted neckerchief round it to hold it in place and the blood would soon stop running and he would carry on as if nothing had happened.

There are many other cures from nature but they are best left untold as some of them involve the use of many poisons found in plants and if not mixed correctly could have serious consequences, so we must let the secret of their use remain with the people who discovered their value.

Chapter 26

My First Real Chance

Back to my lorry days. I found life getting more interesting every day and a few more cars were appearing, such as the bull-nose Morris; there were several of these on the roads. The representative of our Shell Company had one which I admired, never having been close to one before. The Model T Ford was much in evidence and it was not long before many of the tradesmen were replacing their horses and vans for one of these new machines.

The time came for us to take our lorry to Ipswich to have new solid tyres fitted and what a machine it was which did this job. The wheel was taken from the lorry and placed over a pit. The shape of the wheel, a new iron and rubber tyre, was suspended over it and then slowly but surely it was pressed down towards the wheel. As contact was made, a great hissing emerged from the machine as it forced one tyre off as the other took its place. It was all done by water pressure I was told, quite a remarkable machine.

Often we would get stuck when going too close to the edge of the road with these tyres and narrow wheels and would be marooned, sometimes all day, waiting for another of our lorries to return home from its day's work. On arriving back they would receive the message we had sent from the nearest telephone that we were in trouble. One day we were stuck at a farm at 10 a.m. and had to wait until 4.30 p.m. before the farmer would let the engine which was threshing pull us out. It took only a minute but the farmer said time was money and in no circumstances could he stop work to help us, even for a minute. Another occasion was the day we were tangled up with a steam roller. Our front wheels jumped over the chain which was steering the front roller and this severely bent our steering. The roller driver had to dismantle his chain and pull clear of our lorry, which took several hours. There was much swearing all round, until our Rep. turned up in his Morris (he happened to be in the area that day). I think he smoothed things over with the roller driver, promising him something which must have pleased him because all three disappeared into the pub nearby. When they finally came out, the Rep. said to me 'I think I had better help get the lorry home as it will take a bit of steering; you had better drive my Morris, I understand you can drive.' I explained that I had never driven a car before but he said 'Well, if you can drive that lorry you can drive a car. Keep close behind the lorry, we shall only be doing about ten miles an hour. As a matter of fact, if you want I will sell it to you, the company are getting me a new model and I can sell this for £5. It's yours if you want it.' I replied '£5!! Why, I haven't got five shillings. Besides, I daren't let the Squire of my parish or anyone else see me with that, they would think I was acting above my station in life.' He said 'You know best,' and the chance was lost.

The next day, as the lorry was not available, I had to stay at the depot on Victoria Road, painting petrol cans. These were repainted every time they were returned, so as to always look smart, especially if they were strapped to the running board of a posh car. During the morning, my driver and the foreman decided the top depot needed their attention. I wondered if the fact that the depot was situated at the station next to the 'Jolly Porters' pub had anything to do with their sudden desire to pay a visit! I was given the order to answer the telephone should it ring in their absence – I was petrified! I had never been near a telephone, let alone answered one. I asked to be shown what to do and was told how to place the receiver to my ear and answer slowly. I prayed the 'phone would not ring, but ring it did. I went slowly into the office and gingerly lifted the receiver to hear a voice very faintly say 'Hello! Diss! Hello! Diss!' I said words to the effect of why I and not the foreman was answering the telephone and got so excited I gabbled on and on until whoever it was at the other end slammed the telephone down on me. I felt very sorry for myself and did not know what to tell the foreman when he returned. To my relief there were no more telephone calls and when the foreman and my driver returned and asked if anyone had rung, I said 'Yes, but I don't know who, all he kept saying was 'Hello! Diss.' The foreman said 'That would be Head Office, I will ring them to see if the message was important.' Off he went into the office and came back ten minutes later saying 'It was Head Office and they want to know what ** fool they had working for them!' I was a long while living down that experience!

Chapter 27

Changing Scenes

The summers were hot and most nights when leaving work I would cycle to Hoxne river and have a swim before going home for tea. This worried my mother because often I was the only one at the river and the water was deep. I felt I had to keep reassuring myself I could really swim, having only just been taught by the Scouts before I left school. Sometimes there would be several people swimming, showing off their skills at diving and swimming under water. One boy could swim 50 yards under water and he was known as 'Muddy' because he was always covered in mud. We thought he pulled himself along the bottom instead of swimming.

I continually thought to myself what a wonderful world I was living in. This was especially so when I was persuaded to join the 'Imps' Junior Imperial League which was going strong in Diss at that time. This was an organization designed to help young people along the early years of life. Our headquarters were at the old Stay factory in Heywood Road. It became known as the Imps Hut and many a happy hour was spent there. We had our own dance band called 'The Imps' and a very good concert party was formed, known as 'The Imps Concert Party'. It was in great demand, as was the band, and they travelled all over the county, winning many prizes. Mr Harold Jefferies was the backbone of the organization and arranged many outings, the highlight of which was a visit to the Houses of Parliament. After a complete tour of the building, we enjoyed a strawberry tea on the veranda overlooking the Thames. To complete the day, seats were booked for us at the London Palladium to see the first appearance in England of 'Duke Ellington and his Band'. It was the first time we had ever seen such a big band, and the memory of that occasion has remained with me ever since.

The Diss Imps Concert Party.

The sound of the band was still ringing in my ears when I reached home and, feeling very happy, I was not prepared for the news my father had for me. The farm was to be let to someone else, so everything had to be sold, including his beloved horses. The dreadful day dawned when my father had to feed the horses for the last time. They were then tied in a long row across the meadow and each had a lot number stuck on its rump. I think my father and the other horsemen all felt very bad at seeing their animals go to new owners. Some horses were very old and had to be put down but some were still very useful for doing small jobs about the farms. The new owner of the farm came from the Fens area and had completely different methods of farming. He did not require many men as he had working sons of his own and he brought all his own equipment with him, including three or four horses. The tractor was then being used extensively so the writing was on the wall for the horses to go. Only two men were engaged from the large number who were previously employed.

To give some idea of the number of men needed in the early days, I can remember one year in particular when there was a wet harvest and most of the fields of barley were flattened. Whole fields had to be mowed by hand with as many as 28 men working in one field scything, one of the hardest and most skilful jobs. I saw the sweat coming through the backsides of the men's white corduroy trousers until they became black with sweat. No-one could rest until the 'Lord' or leader at the front stopped to sharpen his scythe, when they would all stop and do the same. A sight never to be repeated on such a scale. After the barley was cut, a horse-drawn rake was used to pull it into rows which required turning several times. This was sometimes done by hand, or a toppler was sometimes used. This was a peculiar contraption and took a fair bit of skill to use. Loose barley was the hardest stuff to load on the wagons. Extra-wide forks were used for this and often a wagon had to be roped in several places to hold the load to the wagon. The loose straws would adhere to the hedges, leaving evidence of those passing wagons.

Chapter 28

Crossroads

Although I was at work and away from the farm, my thoughts were never far from the childhood I remembered which was so involved with life on the farm. The news that my father would no longer be a part of it upset me greatly and set me thinking more than ever of the responsibilities falling on my young shoulders. I was now the breadwinner and there was no unemployment benefit. My mother had to manage on the ten shillings (50p) I gave her plus one shilling a week from the club but fortunately these circumstances did not last long as father managed to get a gardening job earning thirty-five shillings a week – five shillings better than before. In a way Mother was glad Father was off the farm and doing a job which did not ruin his health. She said he had done enough 'clodhopping' – a term used for farm workers. I was relieved and went about my job with renewed vigour.

The next change was the appearance of the AA man on his splendid yellow motor cycle frequently passing along the main road. He saluted smartly at some of the cars, which by now had increased in numbers, and I discovered he was saluting the cars which had an AA badge on the front, proving their owners were members of the organization. He could often be seen tinkering with a car or motor cycle by the roadside as part of his duties. The first local patrol man was Bert Tyrel, who also spent a lot of his time directing traffic at the Scole/Diss crossroads as, although there were only a few cars compared to today, cars were considered a danger. He would do the same thing at the Pulham crossroads where after a time the AA installed a smart hut with a telephone. This was a meeting place for all patrols and they made it a showpiece on the main road by creating a very pretty flower garden around it which they lovingly tended. The fascination of the man waving his arm about was such that it became quite a talking point in the pubs. One inmate of the nearby workhouse, known as 'Pulham Union', used to walk to the crossroads when he was allowed out and stand in the middle of the road for hours on end in his white corduroy trousers frantically waving his arms trying to copy the AA man who he had watched in admiration. The motorists got so used to him that they would salute him back.

All the inmates of the workhouse were distinctive by their white corduroy trousers which squeaked when they walked. Workhouses were not the best of homes to live in and could be very cruel, although I suppose the people who administrated them did what they thought was best. Many stories were told of these places but I am only recounting what I know to be the truth in these memories. My great-uncle Jimmy, who lived alone, would sit by his fireside all day smoking an old black pipe, looking at an old black fireplace. He had a white beard which was black with grime but he was happy in his dirt and seemed as strong as a horse, never ailing until he developed a heavy cold which he could not shake off. The doctor was called in and he ordered old uncle Jim to Pulham Union. My mother, who had visited him daily at his home, walked to Pulham and was directed to the ward Uncle was in. She walked past the rows of white-faced old men and could not recognise her uncle. 'He was like a china doll,' Mother said. His beard had been hacked off until his face bled and he had been scrubbed with an ordinary scrubbing brush to get him clean – a regular practice which was used on all the vagrants they had to deal with. Old men had their backsides smacked if they made a mess in the bed, and the women, too. Boys were mixed with the men and the able-bodied were made to dig the huge garden to provide as many vegetables as possible. The women were made to scrub the floors and stairs, which were all stone. It was a hard life there. Following the rough treatment my uncle Jim received, he only managed to live a week. There were no nurses as such; the only staff employed were chosen from the surrounding villages. They were very robust with arms as big as gateposts and could handle the heaviest and most difficult person with ease. They wore sack aprons most of the time. Women who had babies out of wedlock were often banished to the workhouse in shame and many a poor girl would be ruined for life after suffering this humiliation. Few employers would engage a girl with such a background.

Next to this institution stood the Queen's Head public house which is now a private dwelling, which was conveniently put there to entice the spending of the few coppers pocket money the old boys were allowed. Beer was only 2d for a half pint, shag tobacco 3½d for half an ounce and matches ½d per box so 6d (2½p) would gain them admittance. Several escaped to enjoy a rare bit of freedom from the dreaded workhouse but seldom did they have more than a few coppers to spend, it all depended on the job they did to earn a pittance.

Next to the pub was a remand home for wayward boys which always boasted that it was a complete cure for bad boys. Windows were barred and the whole property securely fenced in. A master and his wife lived there to administer whatever punishment was required, which must have had the desired effect as no boy ever returned for a second dose. As I went past this terrible place each week in the company of my friendly driver, George, I used to think of those other poor boys who had experienced part of their lives behind those grim doors and I thought how lucky I was to be in such happy times with my whole life before me.

Although we were poor financially, money did not seem to be the only thing in life then: there were other attractions to look forward to, such as the visit of the fair. Yes, to see the bill announcing the coming of the fair to our local town was like a tonic to us, old and young alike. Everyone would think and talk of nothing else.

'The fair is coming to Diss,' said Leonard.

'Whose fair?' asked Frank.

'Bert Stock's,' replied Leonard.

'I hear he's got a good set of steam horses,' said another voice from the crowd of about a dozen men who had gathered on the corner for their nightly mardle (chat).

'He's got a good steam engine too, I shall have to see that,' said the local engine driver from the farm.

'I like to hear the organ,' said one and 'I like a good old swing on the swinging boats,' said another.

'You don't want to swing!' You only go there so you can see the girls' legs when they stand up showing all their frilly petticoats, that's what you go for. I have seen you staring many a time,' laughed the first.

'Hold your row together,' said Leonard. 'Let's have a game of quoits,' and with that brief interlude of village chat, life would carry on.

To we country folk the fair was magic and people would cycle to Anness Meadow in Diss in their hundreds. All the pubs would do a roaring trade in storing cycles at 2d each. The fairground would be crowded. We all stood and wondered how everything worked. The roundabout was the chief attraction; the horses all beautifully carved and going up and down to the gay music coming from the organ. With all the polished twisted brass and the many electric lights we were at a loss to understand how they managed to light it all up. We were caught in the carnival atmosphere which prevailed, a feeling which seemed to be catching as everyone was so happy. There were no real fights to speak of, only one now and again over a girl, and other boys would stand around and watch, rather than join in as they do today.

The fair would perhaps be at Diss Thursday, Friday and Saturday and at Eye, a distance of six miles, on the following Monday, Tuesday and Wednesday. The reason for the short distance between stops was the need for water. Sometimes a farmer would provide a water cart along the road for the engine to use but there were plenty of ponds close to roads where boilers could be replenished. With our new-found freedom with our bicycles, we would often follow a fair about but we would always respect our parents' wish and not be out after a certain time. We would stop and listen to the fair music on the way home, the tunes we loved gradually getting fainter until we could hear no more. We would have to wait for the fair to return to rekindle that lovely experience.

At fifteen years of age I was experiencing a life I had never previously dreamed existed. I wondered what my school friends were up to. It was strange but the life I had previously lived and the boys and girls I had played with seemed to have vanished for the time being but in the back of my mind I knew everything I had experienced in my early life would stand me in good stead for a future I could not picture, as things were moving so fast. By this time charabancs were a regular sight coming home from a day at the seaside with streamers flying in long tails at the back. These would have been purchased at Woolworths at six for a penny and I think all outings were in competition with each other to see how many streamers they could produce. The passengers sang all the latest songs at the tops of their voices. We were no exception when we had our choir outing and I think we outdid the lot! I remember, too, that I had relations on the way home from Yarmouth who could always expect a stick of rock to be thrown into their garden as we sped past at ten miles per hour! Happy days! All the latest tunes would be whistled by those who could and especially by the errand boys, of whom there were plenty as every shop seemed to employ an errand boy. I used to whistle all the way to work, thinking I was pleasing the people in the cottages I passed, as not all had a wireless set to know what the latest tunes were.

Chapter 29

My World is Shattered

I was a member of the Reading Room in our village and went every night to be with other men and boys, playing games. Upon returning home one fateful night I was confronted by my mother at our doorstep, informing me she thought my father had had a stroke. He was sent to hospital the next day and our worst fears were confirmed.

'He has had a stroke and little hope of recovery can be given.' He was 48 years of age. We put his bed in our front room and there my mother nursed him for the next six years until he died. I do not wish to burden the reader with all the heartaches that went with that experience, which happened in my tender years of adulthood, only to say I then had to adapt to a much restricted way of life. I had to shave my father twice a week and help to wash him. He was a very big man and, being helpless, was too much for my mother to manage alone. The total allowance my mother received was eleven shillings per week which, with my ten shillings, left us well and truly in poverty street. Around this time the Squire's wife died and the whole village mourned her passing. It was snowing heavily on the day of her death but suddenly the weather relented on the day of her funeral and the pall bearers were able to carry her body through the woods and over the park to her resting place and for good measure the sun shone, too. At the time it was said that it was because she had lived such a good life.

'It's an omen' some of the villagers said with awe.

A few months passed and the Hall was deeply concerned about how we were managing to cope, with me away all day and mother having to do everything herself. One day the Squire's daughter, Miss Molly, who was the Scout Mistress, suggested to her father that it would be a good idea if I worked at the Hall in the gardens. I did not like the idea at first but could see the logic in it, so I consented and very reluctantly gave my notice at the

My parents in 1934 (taken by the author with a cheap box camera).

petrol company. I started work for sixteen shillings a week, to be paid once a month. There was no half day, which nearly broke my heart as I would miss my cheap Saturday afternoon at the cinema. Worse was to follow when the Head Gardener's son played cricket on Saturdays and I had to work. Once a month I had to work Sundays, too, watering the greenhouses and attending to the fires. I wondered what I had let myself in for but then I would think of Mother tied to the house day and night and would realize I had nothing to grumble about. As my wages were now slightly higher, I was able to give mother another two shillings a week and have another two for myself, bringing my total pocket money to four shillings per week. Surprisingly enough, this seemed to be enough, as things kept at the same price year in and year out. A new suit could be made to measure for fifty shillings (£2.50), a new bicycle could be purchased for three pounds ten shillings (£3.50) and a tie for one shilling and sixpence (7½p), which seemed to be the most popular Christmas present for men. It was four pence (2p) for a haircut and twopence for a shave (less than 1p). Ladies' hair was left alone or to be in the latest fashion they could pay one shilling (5p) for a 'bob' trim. I think this was the best ladies' hair fashion of all. Maybe it is because I was young at the time.

It was during these early days at the Hall that we first heard of Woolworths at Great Yarmouth and all the things to be purchased at no more than sixpence for the dearest item. As it was getting near the time for our choir outing to Yarmouth, we were all looking forward to seeing what Woolworths was like! We journeyed by charabanc and arrived about three hours later after a journey of 35 miles. Our first impression of the beach was the famous sand models which were a feature of sandy resorts. A product of the First World War, these models were all painstakenly made by hand by ex soldiers, of a fallen horse with its rider kneeling beside it, cap in hand, his puttees realistically reproduced in the sand and his rifle a short distance away. A few words would be formed in the sand, perhaps saying 'Farewell old friend'. This scene brought many a tear to the eyes of the passers by who would throw their odd coppers onto a large tarpaulin near where the artist sat, with a notice saying 'All my own work'. Sadly, with the demise of these old soldiers, that wonderful art has gone forever. We moved on and paid a penny to be weighed on the lovely brass scales and then made a beeline for the Pleasure Beach (fun fair) which to us was a wonderland of rattle and music coming from the tannoy speakers tied to the various rides with string. We could not understand how the music got there but they played our favourite tunes and we felt very happy. We did not spend much as we were saving for the visit to Woolworths and anyway we did not have much to spend; I had saved up six shillings for the outing. We all had to meet at Elise's Restaurant for lunch, which the rector paid for. It was one shilling per head (5p) as there was a party, one shilling and sixpence (7p) for individuals. After our meal we went back to the amusements to watch the various rides, many of which we had never seen the like before. The Caterpillar was one where a cover came over the ride at various times, to plunge the occupants into darkness, this caused much screaming from the girl occupants. We had a few goes at darts at a penny for three and at the hoopla also a penny to throw three hoops. We never won anything! Our mothers had warned us about these stalls, so we were not surprised. At teatime we had a cup of tea at one of the beach stalls for another penny and then went off to Woolworths. The first thing which we saw as we approached the shop was the sign stating nothing was over sixpence in the store. What a sight the store was to us from the country, who had seen nothing larger than our village grocer's shop before. There seemed to be everything one could wish to buy from the smallest screw or nail to a pair of spectacles, which were piled high on the counter. A card was there for the buyer to read when selecting a pair and when he had found a pair which suited then he would pay the smart girl assistant sixpence, and if a case was required a further threepence would be charged. All the other goods were on display, with a girl assistant every ten feet or so who had her particular line to sell, be it a yard of flex or a yard of elastic at 1½d per yard. Pots and pans at threepence each, lids were threepence extra, also knives, forks and spoons at threepence each. A hammer could be bought for sixpence – the hammer head threepence and the handle threepence. I spent most of the money I had left on things for my mother, including a penny mousetrap. We all brought streamers to hang behind the charabanc for the journey home, singing our favourite tunes all the way.

Chapter 30

Pulham Airships and The Owl

I well remember the airship days at Pulham. The huge sheds, or hangars, presented a frightening sight to us as we approached them when a pulling was required. Pulling was the term used when all available people were required to hang onto the long ropes dangling from one of the large airships or 'Pulham Pigs' as they came to be known. As many as 200 or more people would be needed to hold and guide these large ships into the huge hangars. Each hangar stood on four acres of ground. A man would cycle into the surrounding villages shouting the pending arrival of a ship. Word would soon be passed round and all those living near who were available would rush to the hangars. The women would come too, running over the footpaths, jumping the ditches and lifting their long skirts to clear the brambles. It was a rare sight and not only did they get paid for it but everyone living near looked on this as a duty they had to perform to get the airship either in its hangar or hooked to the giant mooring mast. This was where the R33 spent most of its time, with a gun carriage suspended from the stern to keep it parallel. One day in a gale the ship was torn from its mast, taking the heavy carriage with it suspended in the air. It got blown over the North Sea where the crew managed to regain control and bring it safely home where several hundred people, including myself, were waiting to pull. This was a precarious job. If the ship decided to take a sudden lift upwards, we all had to leave go for fear of rising with it. One man grimly held on on one occasion and was soon dangling 100 feet above the ground. Fortunately the ship dropped as suddenly as it had ascended and he dropped off from about ten feet and was unhurt.

While the airships were active at Pulham, several experiments were carried out. One was the carrying of a small aeroplane under the belly of the ship, fixed to a thirty-foot rod. When the ship was about 4,000 feet in

The R33 Airship, attached to its mast, at Pulham Airfield.

the air, the plane was released and would drop like a stone for hundreds of feet, until the pilot took over. He would fly around and then attach the plane back onto the rod under the ship. This required a considerable amount of skill and would be repeated several times during the exercise, much to the horror of all those watching.

'There's no telling where them planes might drop if they fall off,' remarked one woman to my mother, who replied 'They are getting ready for another war. They will be dropping spies over Germany with them little planes. We don't know half what's going on.' Such was the ignorance of the village people. If a stranger was seen walking past, especially when surveying for a new map, word would soon be passed around that there were spies about. People were very suspicious and memories of the last war were slow to fade.

'It scared the life out of me,' said Fred.
'What did?' asked Ted.
'Why, that ruddy owl, all lit up.'
'What do you mean all lit up, and what owl?'
'Well,' explained Fred 'I was biking home to Dickleburgh at about ten o'clock last night when this owl went "whoo whoo" in the rectory garden at Rushall and came flapping straight in front me; and it shone all over, all

lit up like I said. Was I frightened! I fell off my bike while trying to get away from it. I looked round and there it was sitting on the rectory gatepost as if it was on fire.'

'Have you told anybody else yet?' asked Ted, but Fred said 'No, I reckon they won't believe me, but I did see it.'

A few days elapsed, Fred went miles out of his way to get to Rushall such was his fear of going past the rectory. But he was not the only one to see this apparition and it soon became a common sight at nightfall. News of the Rushall luminous owl reached the newspapers and many a story was recorded of sightings. Children were afraid to go out after dark and the Half Moon pub became a centre of local gossip and many a weird and wonderful tale was told about the luminous owl, until suddenly there were no more sightings and people began to wonder if they had imagined the whole thing. A few months after the last sighting, the truth of the matter was revealed. It appeared some airmen stationed at Pulham had captured this owl and painted it with luminous paint, then released it back to its hollow tree where it stayed all day. As owls do, it only came out at night and it presented a fearsome sight! This was in the year 1927, as I remember.

Chapter 31

I Learn the Hard Way

To return to everyday life at the Hall: I was learning the hard way what adult life was all about. I worked in what is best described as a Victorian garden, where many of the old rules remained. Instead of riding round in a petrol lorry all day and having the odd refreshment in a pub passage, I found myself on my hands and knees weeding the paths or scrubbing flowerpots. I was not allowed to do more interesting jobs for several weeks but was soon taught how to dig properly by one of the old hands, who resented anyone else treading on his sacred ground. Consequently, when I appeared on the scene, I was soon made to feel an unwanted outsider, which made me very miserable and I was glad when I was allocated chiefly to work with the Head Gardener's son, who I got on well with. My school pal, Frank Noble, worked with Bill too, in the vegetable garden were they both worked very hard, digging by hand this huge garden which was of very heavy soil. I was soon put to work with them 'to break me in' it was said, and well I knew it! We started at 7 a.m. and worked until 5.30 p.m. with few breaks. I was told 'Keep that back bent, Sidney' every time I tried to pause, until I thought my back would break. I was thinking all the time of the life I had left for this and I reminded myself I was doing this for my mother's sake. I could picture my poor father in bed suffering and thought I must stick it, but the world suddenly appeared to be a cruel place and after my previous carefree ways I began to have doubts. Fortunately, this state of affairs did not last long and the pleasures of my former life gradually faded. I began to realize what a lot of wonderful things there were here for me to appreciate and be thankful for.

There were five gardeners: Arthur Gibson (Head), William Gibson, William Nunn, Frank Noble and myself. In the house were W W Sargent (Chef), A Knight (Butler) and five maids. Outside were the electrician,

Reg Warnes and S Cattermole, the chauffeur and F Hubbard was Boot Boy. That was the complete private staff to the Squire and his family in 1930.

Gamekeepers were never far away; they seemed a suspicious breed of people, always popping up where you least expected. They had an important job on the estate as the game were Sir Edward's pride and joy; everyone and everything revolved round the game. They were never to be frightened or disturbed in any way and when the hayfields were cut, if a nest was in the way, it had to be left. Many a tuft of grass would be left to hide a nest. It seemed the keepers had a sixth sense – if a nest was in your garden, they would soon relieve it of the eggs and take them to the Hall for the Chef to use. We had a single barrel shotgun in the garden to shoot bullfinches and vermin which did harm to the trees. When we killed anything, we had to lay it out for Sir Edward but before he saw it, a keeper would appear from nowhere to make sure we had shot vermin and nothing else. They certainly did the job they were paid to do. Sir Edward was a very kind and placid gentleman normally, but the one thing that would arouse his anger was if he had had a report from one of his keepers that game stocks were not as high as they should be. This information would certainly set him going, and woe betide the first person he saw after such news. He was more concerned that the gentlemen he invited to his shoots should have a good day's sport and he gave them all the best positions while he himself followed the beaters and shot the odd water hen or rabbit. On a good day some 800 birds would be shot and several rabbits. While working in the garden this sounded like a battlefield around us. Sometimes a pheasant would fall in the gardens but a keeper would be there before we finished work, using his uncanny skills in sniffing out the game! 'Wanted it for the count,' he would say.

We once had a cock pheasant in the garden which was becoming a pest. It would peck flowers up and play havoc with young plants but we dare not shoot it. When we told the keeper about it he said 'They do no harm, leave it alone.'

'We soon won't have anything left,' replied the Head Gardener.

'Tell Sir Edward then,' challenged the keeper. The gardener retorted that he would, but he was very reluctant to do so for fear of what Sir Edward might say. The opportunity arose when the Squire was looking at the damage to his flowers and asked what was the cause.

'I am glad you asked,' said Arthur. 'It is a pheasant, a cock pheasant.'

'What!' shouted the Squire. 'Don't tell me such rubbish, pheasants don't do that sort of damage! It's a rabbit; you've got a gun, shoot it,' and with that he stormed off, leaving poor Arthur to reflect on the wisdom of having said anything in the first place. About a fortnight later, the Squire was again in the garden. He happened to look in   the direction of the flower border and there, as large as life, was the cock pheasant, tearing at the flowers and pulling them up by the roots. He could hardly believe what he had seen and quickly returned to the Hall to fetch his gun but when he returned the pheasant had gone. Sir Edward found Arthur and told him 'You can shoot that pheasant, it's a rogue, that one. That one only, mind you. Then take it to Sargent (the chef).' With that he strode off without saying another word.

Little episodes like that were not often repeated as we all seemed to work within the laws of the establishment. We had the feeling of being one big family but at the same time there was always the fear of putting one step out of place and being for the high jump. This was the result of the Victorian age just past, when servants were servants in the true sense of the word.

With the coming of the wireless and motor travel available to a lot more of the general public, we who lived in the age of change and worked in a village such as ours appreciated this new-found freedom opening up before us. We could now catch a bus at our gate, although it was a bumpy ride. However, bicycles were the chief method of transport and were put to all sorts of uses. One such was the coming of the 'Stop me and buy one' ice-cream cycle – a large box container attached to a three-wheeler cycle with the two wheels at the front taking the weight of the ice cream which Walls sent daily by train to stations from where the ice-cream men would cycle to the surrounding villages. At the end of their day's selling, they would return to the nearest station and discuss with each other the day's business and who had the best round, before entering the guard's van with their cycles. Ices would be 1d and 2d (less than 1p) and if a larger quantity was required, people would take a basin out to the cycle to have it filled. It became a common sight to see these blue boxes saying 'Stop me and buy one' trundling around the countryside.

The Hall, in common with other large estates, was reluctant to accept the time of change which was upon us, but bow to it they did. The first change was the five and a half day week – how we appreciated that! Even so, there were snags for gardeners as we had to shut the greenhouses up at night and water and stoke the fire in the winter. This we took turns to do. Life carried on at a leisurely pace but now, instead of hearing only the sound of men shouting at their horses in the distance, we heard the sounds of tractors which were being used in ever increasing numbers. To us it was dreadful that the noise of these machines should wreck our once peaceful countryside.

'It won't get any better,' said Arthur. 'Anyway, it won't be so hard for the horses.'

'Ah!' said Ted. 'But look how these old wheels are going to firm the land down. Horses know where to put their feet, a tractor don't.'

'Them that live the longest will see the most,' mused Arthur and with that exchange of views work was resumed.

The next change at the Hall was the installation of a petrol pump for their private use. It became very difficult to store enough petrol in cans to keep the cars going, so a personal pump was the sensible thing to have. The Squire's son insisted. Sir Edward still craved for the return of his beloved horses but he knew that would never be and he reluctantly agreed for the pump to be installed. He hated the internal combustion engine and so when the tank arrived one of his workmen was instructed to dig this enormous hole by hand. It happened to be in the middle of a heatwave when this unfortunate man was digging in the heavy soil and so he was soaked in sweat and desperate for a drink. The Butler went past with a jug of beer for a man who was harrowing the meadow with horses, but on the instructions of the Squire no beer was offered to him. Sir Edward sympathised with the horseman but had no time for a man working twice as hard digging a hole for a petrol tank for those 'confounded combustion engines'.

The Diss Horticultural Summer Show was always held on the Rectory Meadow near the Church School. This involved us in a lot of extra work which we enjoyed. We would be in competition with Major Denny of Garboldisham Manor and Miss Pauline of Thorpe Abbotts; a friendly rivalry existed between the sets of gardeners. This was repeated in the Autumn when a Chrysanthemum Show was held in the Corn Hall at Diss and although competition was keen, we had a good result each year. In the latter years before the Second World War, Scole Paddocks entered the field with A Ellinor as Gardener. They gave us a good run for our money and beat us on several occasions, which did not go down very well with our boss. However, he was always proud of his garden and each year in May, when the Diss Horticultural Society visited the gardens, he would issue a challenge to everyone who came. He offered a pound to anyone who could find a weed – nobody ever claimed!

While at work, many topics would be discussed which had been heard on the wireless the night before. This was the chief interest to us all in those early days of radio and what a kick we got if we were able to tell our

Prize blooms at Thelveton Hall.

friends something they had not heard, especially if a new tune was played for the first time. We used to say 'Have you heard the latest tune?' and we would whistle it as best we could. I well remember 'Painting the Clouds with Sunshine' and 'Tip toe Through the Tulips' being all the rage and hearing the massed bands of the Scottish Troops playing these tunes as they marched from Diss Station to Hoxne Park where they had a brief stay. People for miles around visited their camp when it was open to the public for displays of marching and displays from the cavalry. There seemed to be hundreds of horses, a sight few who witnessed this event will forget. I mention this as we were privileged to see such things right in our midst.

It was around this time I experienced my first visit to a dentist. I had a very bad tooth which needed pulling and I plucked up courage and cycled to Diss where I saw the dentist who was an elderly man who came daily by train from Norwich. I was his first 'victim' of the day. He had just recovered from a severe bout of flu and was very weak. I had very large-rooted teeth and he found it almost impossible to get my tooth out. He pulled and pushed, twisted and turned, lifting me off my seat at times, and I screamed with fear and pain. He had to have a rest and then had a second try, much to my apprehension. There was more twisting and screaming. I was really scared when with an awful crack the tooth gave way. The dentist was dripping with sweat and said 'I knew I should not have come today, I am not fit.' With that he sat down, looking worse than I did. He thrust a glass of water into my hands to rinse my mouth, then collapsed again, repeating 'I wish I had stayed at home.' He gave me my tooth, which had three fangs, all twisted, for me to keep, saying 'If you get the toothache again, you had better go to a younger man. You Norfolk people are all alike, no wonder they call you Swede Bashers!' I cycled home feeling very sorry for myself, spitting blood all the way and wanting to meet someone I knew to proudly show them the tooth I had just had extracted. It became quite an obsession for days as all I wanted to do was show off this tooth, it being a new experience for me. I had many more experiences of a similar nature as my teenage years sped by and by the time I was 21 years of age I had lost all my teeth and was proudly showing off the false set which now made all the difference. I could eat properly and smile, showing off my nice white teeth and not the awful ones I had before.

We were all a little vain and were very particular how we dressed. Our trousers had to have a sharp crease at all times, shoes had to be brightly polished and we always wore a tie on Sundays and special occasions. Trousers were the only garment which altered to any extent over the years, sometimes 18" bottoms were all the fashion, then extra-wide bottoms, once getting to 28". Square shoulders became all the rage when the gangster films were shown and to copy Al Capone, suits had padding fitted in the shoulders. Mine was no exception, it was a smart fashion and a brand new suit would cost from £2 10s (£2.50), while casual flannel trousers were from 5s (25p) to 12s (60p). Shoes were from 4s 6d (22p) up to 12s, depending upon the quality.

Chapter 32

The Garden of Eden

'Let's go to the Garden of Eden,' said Frank, my workmate.

'Garden of Eden?' I asked. 'Where's that?'

Frank explained about the lovely garden a postman had created at Banham out of the disused brick workings. There were huge hollows left after they finished extracting the clay when the Banham brickyard ceased making the famous Banham red bricks. Some of these crater-like holes were twenty feet deep. There were hills and hollows, mounds and flat

The Garden of Eden.

areas which this postman had transformed into a place of beauty in his spare time. It took years to create.

'Let's go. Now we've got good cycles we can go anywhere,' said Frank.

We arranged to go the following Sunday after church. We dare not miss church as although we were in our teens we were still living in Thelveton and under the influence of the strict rules of the Hall regarding Sunday, and how it should be spent.

We started our journey after lunch and although only about eight miles, it seemed as if we were embarking on a round-the-world trip. Until then, travelling to the next village seemed like visiting another world. We marvelled at other people's houses and gardens on the way, all the time hoping we would not get a puncture, so we could get home safely. We could mend punctures should we have to, but we always feared the worst about getting stranded miles away from home; the world seemed a big place to us in the early thirties. As we pedalled on, Frank remarked on the possibility of meeting some girls there. It seemed there was a tunnel cut right through one of the mounds which was known as 'The tunnel of love'. Quite an exciting place we were visiting, according to Frank!

When we arrived, we were amazed to see such a smart new chalet-type house standing at the entrance to this abandoned site, apparently in the

The Garden of Eden.

middle of nowhere. In the lounge of the house a man was in charge of selling picture postcards. Lemonade from a large demi jar was also for sale at 1d per glass. The jars were very popular and could be seen in most village shops in the local area. The lemonade was homemade from lemon crystals. As the whole area was the property of the Rout family who manufactured cider, bottles of their famous cider were on sale, also crisps. No one lived in the house, as a buyer could not be found at that time, so it was known as 'The White Elephant' and was just used for storage or as a shelter for visitors, should it rain. A small fee of 3d (1p) was charged for admittance, which was for the upkeep of the garden. There was also a box for donations to the postman who did all the work himself; and what an achievement it was!

Going down the steps into the garden one was confronted with a long grass path. The garden was full of surprises, around every corner a breathtaking view was revealed of flower borders of every colour, cleverly mingling with the profusion of fruit bushes and trees. There were scores of apple trees trained as cordons, the first I had seen trained this way. They were heavy with fruit but despite the many visitors and its isolation, we were told that seldom was any fruit taken. Visitors came from all over the world and as news of the 'Garden of Eden' spread, it became quite a

The Garden of Eden.

tourist attraction. Proof of the visitors from far away was in the hundreds of signed names and places written all over the white ceiling at the entrance to the tunnel of love. I even saw one from Hong Kong! Many people came by charabanc as it was a favourite place to visit when on a mystery tour. Of course cycles were the main means of transport but visitors also travelled by car and there was the odd horse and carriage. These were parked in a nearby meadow. Everyone seemed to be so carefree and treated the gardens with such respect, and praise was passed around of the achievements of this one man.

I will try to describe it in more detail as best I can. The main feature of the garden was the clever way the framework of a German zeppelin, shot down nearby during the First World War, was used to make bridges across the hollows and huge overhead trellis work. This structure was used to train apples and other fruit and shrubs under which the visitors strolled in wonder. It was a truly remarkable sight and having visited the gardens once, one felt the desire to visit time and time again. There was a dove cote set amongst the fruit trees and to see these lovely white birds flying around in such a peaceful setting was a joy to all. A huge grape house adjoined the garden, although this was not a part of the Garden of Eden but was owned by the Rout family.

The Garden of Eden.

When we had walked round several times, Frank and I decided to buy drinks and some cards as a reminder of our visit. Then we 'hit the road' for home. We were full of excitement and could talk of nothing else all the way home and decided we would return to this wonderful garden many more times. This we did, along with hundreds of others as it was always such a delight to all.

Alas, it died with the postman as no one would take it on after his death. Anyway, I doubt if anyone could have kept that wonderful atmosphere going for ever.

As for the girls Frank had described on the way, we were much too interested in that wonderful garden! There would be another time perhaps and anyway, we would have been much too shy to approach them as teenagers were like that in those times!

Chapter 33

Village Harvest

The highlight of every Parish was the Harvest Thanksgiving service. On the Saturday preceeding the Sunday of the service, helpers gathered to decorate the church. The entrance lobby would be full of pails and other containers full of Michaelmas daisies, large dahlias and chrysanthemums. Inside on the pews there would be loads of vegetables and fruit – heaps of carrots, lots of special potatoes, large onions, white leeks and bunches of beetroot, cabbages, cauliflowers and parsnips and extra-large marrows. From the Hall garden we would take the best of everything we had and the Head Gardener would always supply the largest bunch of grapes which would be placed on the front of the pulpit after a local farmer had fixed his sheaves of corn. Then there would be the local baker with his loaf of bread shaped like a sheaf of corn. The lady helpers would be busy snipping and tying the flowers at the ends of the pews. The windowsills would be covered with moss and vegetables placed on top to complete the display. At last, everything was in place, the pails were emptied and all the loose petals swept up and everyone went home, satisfied at a job well done.

Sunday arrived and the service was at 3 p.m All who were able were expected to be there, the only time some of the parishioners attended church except for a funeral. As I was in the choir, I could see any new faces and it was always a pleasure to see those men of the land with their Sunday suits on with their watchguards across their fronts; and could they sing! Their rich voices sounded strong and clear above the rest of the congregation offering their thanks for such a bountiful harvest. Although they were 'rough and ready' all year round, they were very genuine in their beliefs and would sing their praises and mean it.

One of my saddest moments in writing these memories is the thought of all the friends and neighbours who would be at the Harvest Thanksgiving but who then passed on during my young days. People seemed to die much younger then and anyone who reached the age of 70 was thought to be very old, due no doubt to the very hard conditions in which they lived. It was normal to leave school at 9 and go straight onto the land to work and the girls went into service at the age of 11. There was no other choice and medicine was not so advanced then.

Chapter 34

Primitive Times

When I arrived home each dinner time and each afternoon there were always jobs waiting to be done.

The first was always to go to the well and fetch the water – not an easy job and it could be a bit nerve-racking looking down that deep hole in the ground at the water far below. Having cranked up a full pail, you had to lean over and lift it up and onto the wooden side of the well, hold it steady while you took the snack off, then lift the pail to the ground without spilling water over your legs. When this was successfully achieved the two large pails had to be carried all the way home.

The next job would be to bury any rubbish of the day such as cinder dirt, slops and empty jars. There were no rubbish collectors and every cottage had to dispose of everything the best way they could. I used to dig a very large hole, about four feet deep and five feet wide. This would last about three months, when another one would be dug. Some people preferred to dig one every day. This practice was repeated over the whole of the county as no one collected anything for you until much later in the 1930s. There were many valuable curios and antiques buried in the gardens in those days. I buried a valuable antique gramophone, which I regret to this day.

I then had to help mother to lift my father so she could either change the sheets or wash him. As previously stated, I shaved him twice a week. A bath chair was on loan from the Hall so when the weather was suitable I could push my invalid father round the village in the Summer evenings and on Saturday afternoons. This I did until I was 21 years of age when my father passed on.

Mind you, it was not all work and gloom, I found time to have a fair bit of leisure away from the house. As my story continues all will be revealed!

Chapter 35

The Lighter Side

The largest circus ever to visit Diss was that of Lord George Sangers. I should think nearly everyone for miles around attended, such was this attraction. From Diss it went on to Harleston and then Great Yarmouth where we lost track. We would take great interest in all fairs and circuses, as they brought much appreciated pleasure to our everyday lives.

Another eagerly awaited event was the Annual Dickleburgh Sport and Horse Gymkhana held every Whit Monday. It was not so much the main events which excited us as the presence of Bert Stock's fair which again would be talked about for many weeks preceeding the event; over 5,000 sixpenny tickets would be sold before the day. I have known people to cycle over 15 miles to come to this event. There would be at least 300 cycles parked in the hedges by the roadside and I can honestly say I never knew of anything being stolen from these bicycles, despite there being good raincoats strapped on the handlebars, for instance. Sometimes, though, when you returned to your cycle, you would find your carbine lamp had been replaced, maybe by a much better one than the one you arrived with. But the replacement would have no carbine in it so you had to walk home. This did not cause too much concern, especially if the replacement was a better one than your original. But it was known that if you took this lamp to enough venues, eventually you may well finish up with the lamp you had in the first place with all the swapping going on. We were used to this crafty honesty.

After the Sports, a dance took place in the Dickleburgh school room where 'Bill Smith's Band' from Pulham Market would be in attendance. Apart from the Diss Imps Band, this was one of the most popular bands at that time. The dances were very popular and in this age of chivalry boys always asked the girls 'May I have the pleasure of this dance?' The girl would probably blush, especially if it was the boy she had had her eyes on and was hoping he would ask her to dance. Yes, everything was very different then. The girls wore long evening dresses which they brought with them to the daytime festivities, ready to change. The boys would carry dance shoes, called pumps, in their saddlebags. Girls and boys vied with one another as to who would look the smartest and I must say that looking back I have yet to see anyone surpass the smartness of the teenagers of those years. I don't know why, when we became adults, we were called 'squares' by the modern youth. However, time marches on and possibly the youth of today will be known by some weird name by a future generation. Who knows?

Train travel was a popular form of transport, especially when cheap excursions were on offer. Trips to London were often arranged when a return ticket cost five shillings (25p). The 200-mile round trip was always arranged for a Sunday and a very long train would be packed. On other occasions a trip would be arranged for a Saturday evening to see a special show in Great Yarmouth for 9d return (less than 4p). This was an 80-mile round trip and needless to say this train would also be packed. This gave us youngsters the chance to see many of the top bands of the day including Billy Merrin, Jack Hilton, Jack Payne and Nat Gonella, to name but a few. Train travel was also made popular with the introduction of holiday runabout tickets which cost ten shillings for a week's travel. You could travel as far as Felixstowe to Sheringham, Cromer and Lowestoft, Great Yarmouth, Norwich and Ipswich, and all stations in between, as many times as you wished during the week of issue. This was very popular. My friend Frank and I once spent a whole day travelling backwards and forwards between Felixstowe and Cromer, travelling several hundreds of miles. We arrived home on the midnight mail train but felt we had had our money's worth!

It was on one of our outings to Great Yarmouth that we had the pleasure of being two of the first passengers on the new scenic railway at the Pleasure Beach funfair. We had looked forward to this for a long time, having read it was to be the largest in England. We had read 'Experience the 60-foot drop on this mile a minute ride' so you can imagine how we felt as we arrived at the Pleasure Beach and first saw this wonderful scenic ride. We were very nervous at first and held very tightly as we were hauled to the top on the click-clacking car. On reaching the top we were more nervous than ever, knowing we could not get out and must face the unknown, which included the awesome 60-foot drop. However, all the other passengers seemed even more frightened than us. We hovered before racing round the first bend to be confronted with a yawning chasm to which we hurtled at great speed. This was it – we plunged down at greater speed than ever, with everyone screaming. Safely out of that scare we rushed around the remaining track taking a few more ups and downs before returning to the start, feeling a wonderful glow of achievement. Before we had time to get off, an attendant was shouting 'Repeat rides only 3d – stay in your car'. We did just that and stayed in the car for 15 rides before calling it a day. We thought we were the pioneers of something special and could not get home fast enough to tell of our great experience, something new to add to our life of discovery.

Chapter 36

Looking Back

As Autumn drew near, I remembered my school days and thought it was coming to the time for pop guns when acorns were used for ammunition. I will try to explain how a pop gun is very simply made. We would first find a piece of elder wood about one foot long and two inches in diameter. Then, with a red-hot iron (we used a poker from the fireplace) we burnt out the centre pith. We then made a plunger from a piece of ash or similar wood which would fit the hole in the elder, shaped to leave a two inch stop at one end. The other end would be wetted and tapped until a brush effect was made. We would then bite an acorn in half, force this into the hollow gun until it reached the far end and the other half of the acorn would be rammed into the other end. The plunger would be forced in and, holding it against our chests and pushing with all our might, the first acorn would be forced out with a loud bang, leaving the second acorn to take the place of the one just fired. It was a simple, hand-made toy which gave a lot of pleasure.

Although I, like all others of my age, was growing up fast into this new world, I often thought back to my school days and remembered the changing seasons for games. There seemed to be a season for pop guns, then hoop bowling would be all the go. This was a round hoop made by the local blacksmith complete with a handle, all made from steel, called a skimmer. How fast we used to bowl along those roads. Then there were the spinning tops made to spin with a stick with a piece of string tied to it with a lash at the end. They could really travel if hit right. This sport had to be abandoned with the increase of traffic and it never returned. There was a season of marbles, then hopscotch, we would be all be able to join in. Another game was tip cat which was not popular in our day but was very popular in our fathers' time.

On arrival at the Hall at 7 a.m. one morning I met the sweep from Diss. He had just swept the massive Hall chimneys and had been there since 4 a.m. This was a once-a-year job. His pony and cart was laden with several sacks of soot which he collected all winter to sell to the farmers for the land in the spring. He used to spread the soot by hand himself and what a dirty job it was. It is the memory of him which prompts me to tell you a few true stories from my earlier childhood associated with the sweep.

When leaving the Hall, he always managed to work a few more cottages in on his way home. He would leave his horse to graze on the grass verge while he swept the cottage chimneys. As there was little or no traffic about in the early 1920s it was quite safe to do this and often the horse would wander quite a distance. One day the sweep was returning to his cart from the cottages when he realized his horse had disappeared. However, he was not prepared for the sight which confronted him when he found his horse. It had its backside high in the air, facing him through a hedge! Whilst grazing, it had backed the cart with its heavy load of soot into a deep ditch, causing the horse to be lifted up, where it hung suspended by its harness. The sweep had to cut the harness to let the horse down, and unload all his soot, then he had to make haste to repair the harness with string, before reloading and returning home.

My mother would always shut up her hens if she knew the sweep was coming as the sight of the brushes shooting out of the chimneys would petrify them and put them off laying for several days.

The sweep from Diss could throw his voice up the chimney and, before he started, he would always ask if I had been a good boy. If mother said no and told him what I had done, before he finished, he would shout from a great height, saying 'Tell that boy Sidney I will come down after him if he isn't a good boy to his mother'. This frightened us children so much we were good for a long time afterwards and for a long time we would look up the chimney to see if we could see anybody.

Chapter 37

Things Move Into a New Era

When we were first able to have a wireless set with a loudspeaker, my father who was ill in bed could not come to terms with how it worked. I used to put it on for him and his eyes lit up with wonderment. His mind was still full of horses. This was reflected one day when Sandy McPherson was playing the organ. At the end as the music faded, my father said 'I reckon he has gone away in a horse and cart!'

To us young ones in those days of the 30s it was work, then music and dancing and looking back I think we had the very best tunes to sing and dance to. Every week there would be a new tune for us to whistle. Love songs and ballads were written by the score. There were real words and meaning to every number and if you whistled or sang any of these songs to your girlfriend she would know it was meant for her, such was the sincerity of the song and the person who sang it. These were wonderful days when people were poor but happy.

We enjoyed the cheap train trips, especially to Norwich to watch the 'Canaries' play football. On the return trip from one such match I was in the train with Charles Steward who was the son of one of the Squire's gamekeepers, and another boy from Thelveton Hall, Ernest Algar from Scole. We got talking about various things and eventually music crept into the conversation, chiefly about dance bands in the area. One of us said 'How about us starting up a band?'

'Although I can play the piano by ear,' said Ernest, 'I would rather play an accordion.' Francis Hubbard said 'I've got one, I think its a good idea. What about you playing the piano, Charles?' Charles asked 'Who is going to play the drums?' and I said 'I can play a bit, my friend Ronnie taught me to play on his and I am willing to give it a go.' So the idea was hatched. Ernest said 'I expect Mother won't mind us practising at our house; we have a piano,' and I added 'I think I know where I can get a cheap set of drums, I hear the Victorians are selling theirs.' So a practice was arranged for two weeks time to allow me time to get the drums, which incidentally cost fifteen shillings (75p). They were only small but they served our purpose well. So the whole thing was arranged on the train between Norwich and Diss.

The year was 1934 when we had our first practice at Bungay Road, Scole, the home of Mrs Alger whose son was the instigator of the band. By this time Ernest had purchased his accordion. We were very nervous at first but as Charles was a pianist who could read music, we felt our confidence growing and were determined to make a go of this enterprise!

It was not long before word got around of what we were up to and many a person had doubts about us making a success of it. Some even said we should have our brains tested to think we could compete with the other bands, while many gave us complete confidence and said 'Good Luck'. After a few weeks of practice, we found that being in a band was not just learning to play. Music had to be purchased and although very cheap at sixpence a copy, it proved to be very costly to provide enough music for four to five hour's playing – roughly 50 to 60 separate tunes would be needed to start with and as the new tunes came out these had to be added. Sometimes there were three or four new tunes in one week and we boys were still only earning about £1 per week. After about six weeks practising, we decided to try our luck as a band and we named ourselves 'The Hall Boys Accordion Band' as three out of the four members worked at the Hall. We then had to decide what to charge if the first two engagements were successful. We decided to offer our services free for the first two engagements, one at Scole and one at Thelveton, after which the charge would be £1 10s for four hours playing and less for whist drives and dances when we would only charge £1 5s. This was for the whole band to share.

Bert Leveret was the first organizer to engage us at the Scole Church Hall for a social and this was a complete success, a forerunner of many such events. Bert was an excellent MC and also a good singer, his rendering of Burlington Bertie will always be remembered by those of us present at that time. Entry to the social was 9d from 7.30 p.m. till 12 midnight. We received five shillings each, plus one shilling which I gave to my cousin for the use of his trailer which went behind my bicycle. This method of transport for the drums and accordion was to last for years, although as we became more popular and in greater demand we would hire Reg Hill, the butcher from Scole, to take us and our supporters on longer distances. He

The Hall Boys Accordian Band 1935. L to R: Jack Thrower; Author; Ernest Alger; Charles Stewart.

would make two journeys at a charge of ten shillings and this would often be a twenty-mile round trip. We completed our first two engagements and fortunately seemed to be a success. We then decided we wanted a better set of drums so Charles, who at that time was in a better-paid job, kindly offered to lend us the money to purchase a larger and better set through the advertising columns of one of the music magazines. We obtained a very good second-hand set from one of the big bands in London. The cost was £8, delivered by rail to my door, the name of the set was 'Premier' and was I proud of this! I lost no time in assembling them on arrival home from work. My mother was in a rare old state seeing these in her house, saying 'Whatever will they say at the Hall? You will get wrong. They will say they are paying you too much.' But I explained Charles had paid for them and that we would pay him back from engagements.

It was a long while before my parents got used to the idea. Time had changed and I, their son, had changed with them. There was no going back to the old quiet ways we were brought up in. I admit I felt a bit apprehensive when we first appeared with the new set-up. By this time we had a uniform of shot silk blouses, black trousers and a waist belt also of shot silk and we looked very smart.

Unfortunately, Francis decided to leave the band for private reasons and so we had to look for another accordionist. Another Scole boy by the name of Jack Thrower was only too pleased to join us and so we were soon practising regularly at Mrs Alger's house in Scole. The neighbours got used to hearing us play as did other people who would often stop outside to listen.

Our very first proper engagement was at Dickleburgh when we played at a whist drive dance organized by Mr Alfred Locket. As might be expected, we were nervous, but everything turned out fine and that same evening we were booked for a return visit. This cheered us up considerably – we were in business!

After this send-off we soon became the talking point of local people; after all, what else was there to do but talk about what was going on locally, especially anything new like a band being formed in their midst. Comments were heard such as 'Unthinkable, whatever next?' 'They won't last long,' and 'They won't like it at the Hall, they can't burn the candle at both ends. Work will suffer, you'll see.' But work didn't suffer as we seemed able to call upon extra reserves of energy in those early days of our lives. Life had taken on a new meaning for me and although I still had to do the same duties at home like shaving my father twice a week and helping Mother all I could, I now had the added interest of looking forward each day to the next band engagement.

As to what the Hall thought, it turned out to be favourable, so we heard from the Butler. Anyway, when the Jubilee celebrations took place, the Squire and his son both made it their business to come and see and hear us at Scole. The Squire said to me the next day 'Well done, Sidney,' and this made me feel very proud of our efforts. On that Jubilee Day in 1935 there were not enough bands to satisfy all the needs of the many villages who were celebrating. We played at Scole for the children at teatime, then went back to Thelveton for tea at 5.30 p.m., and then we cycled back to Scole Church Hall for the rest of the evening's festivities. Quite a day but one I will never forget. Many good tunes had been written by then. I especially remember 'Easter Bonnet' which was very popular and, of course, we had all the Fred Astaire and Ginger Rogers dance numbers to choose from. There were also Cole Porter's many hits. We certainly were living in a happy and exciting era!

Chapter 38

Rumblings of War

People all over the world in the year of 1936 were in a carefree mood and I was enjoying the good life which our limited resources allowed. The news that Germany was re-arming fast sent cold shivers down the backs of the learned ones who had experienced this before and conveyed to me that all was not as well as we tended to believe. I began to wonder whether our lovely band days were going to continue. To add to all these fears a new type of aeroplane was making regular appearances in our skies.

'Whatever sort is it?' I asked someone and was told it was a bombing plane. It was a twin-engine aeroplane and I had never seen one quite like it, as up to now all the planes had single engines.

'There's a war coming,' we were told. This put a whole new outlook on my world. Just as we had accepted the new invention of television the previous year and thought this the ultimate in home pleasure, here we were thinking about a war. These thoughts occupied my mind a great deal and I was shaken by the thought that I might be called up should this war really develop. We tried to put the thought of war to the backs of our minds and things carried on as before. We worked, danced and sang as before, the fairs came with welcome regularity, giving us the exhilaration of the sound of the organ playing the latest tunes. Two which stick in my mind were 'I can't give you anything but love, baby' and 'There's a good time coming'. Of course there were many more, but those two meant a lot to me in those tender years. In our band we had our favourites and the whole world shared these numbers which included 'Who's taking you home tonight?', 'Charmaine', 'Memories', 'Margie', 'Whispering', 'Always', 'Bye bye blackbird' and many more, which were played with feeling and were a joy to play. I think we were very honoured to be part of the generation who were born in this era, as I feel there can never be a better time than that experienced by all of us who lived when all this was happening.

Another year passed before the danger of war again made itself heard, this time we were told volunteers were required to form a civil defence for the whole country in the event of war. This really got us talking, especially when out of the blue a dummy appeared in Mr Hopgood's (of Diss) shop window dressed in full battle dress, complete with gas mask and tin hat. This looked a fearsome sight, hundreds of people stared at it having never before seen anything like it. There was a caption near the model saying 'Modern war dress could look like this. Be prepared, enrol now in the Civil Defence of this Country, should war come, train now!' This put more fear into the locals, including me, and we thought this is it, we must think of what we would like to do. I decided I would like to be a Fireman, while my friends all chose something else. Once enrolled as a Diss Auxiliary Fireman, training began on what we were to expect in the event of war. Gas and its accompanying horrors were to be the first danger to be dealt with. Mr Ralph Bobby of Diss was the chief instructor. He held classes in the Scole Church Hall and was most efficient in his methods of training. Although most people were training for something, life went on in its old sweet way, and our band was still playing in nearly every school and village hall within a twelve-mile radius of Diss. We still practised regularly at Mrs Alger's home at Scole and I feel she deserves a special mention as I know how she enjoyed doing all she could for people. Nothing was ever too much trouble for her. However late we arrived at her house she would produce a hearty meal from somewhere with a smile. Most villages had someone like her who were called upon to undertake all sorts of unpleasant jobs such as being a midwife one moment and laying someone out another; taking in washing and sitting with the sick. I mention this because we had one such person in our village by the name of Mrs Buck who was on hand the day my father died. I am not going to relate all the sad details of that awful day, it would do no good. All I am prepared to say is this happened when I was 21 years of age so I will leave you to guess how I felt. I was left alone with my mother to face the world and its by now uncertain future.

Every year Diss staged a gymkhana followed by a dance in the King's Head Ballroom and a band was always engaged. From this engagement several bookings would follow, including the Banham Pavilion which was the mecca of dance halls in this area, and was renowned for its Saturday night 'hop', as dances were known. There would be several coaches from

Norwich and surrounding towns and there would be cycles by the hundred stacked near the hedges leading to the village. Top bands of the county would be booked with the best local talent, so when we were asked to play there it was the ultimate of our ambitions, although we still had the happiest memories of playing at Scole Church Hall, our first and home ground, so to speak.

Looking back to those happy days, I often think of what lengths we went to to fulfil our engagements. I used to work hard all day, perhaps digging in the gardens at the Hall, from 7 a.m. until 5.30 p.m., go home, have tea, wash, get changed and fetch the trailer from half a mile away. I would then load it with the instruments and leave with the bicycle and trailer and sometimes cycle ten miles to where we were due to play, in every sort of weather. I would start half an hour ahead of the others as I had to walk up the hills, and it could be a very lonely ride sometimes, down the country lanes with the wind howling and the rain or snow beating on my face and the leaves rustling in the hedgerows. It was even worse on the return journey in the early hours of the morning, arriving home at anytime between 1 a.m. and 2.30 a.m., depending on how long we had played. For this night's work we usually received five shillings each, out of which we would purchase a raffle ticket and pay a share to some new music. On arrival home I had to unload the instruments without disturbing my parents who were sleeping in the front room due to my father's illness. I then returned the trailer to where it had been borrowed from. By this time I was often very wet and tired. I would tumble into bed, only to be woken again at 6.30 a.m. by my mother saying 'Time you was up, don't be late for work'. I never was, all the time knowing that the same routine would be repeated that night, so I could not get an early night. Although we tried not to take engagements on consecutive nights, it had to happen sometimes. I remember when Ernie's sister Doris was married, we were engaged to play at the reception on the Saturday, after being out every night the previous week. I had told my mother not to wake me on Sunday morning but to let me sleep. She did not wake me until the Monday morning at 6.30 – I had slept right through the Sunday and Sunday night without waking. Anyway, I was five shillings better off. How different it is today with all the car transport and high fees which can be demanded! Those days were the best days of my young life despite the difficulties with little financial reward. We were rewarded with the friends we made who made up for all the shortcomings experienced in other directions.

Chapter 39

Let's Be Having You

By now the papers were appealing for volunteers for all sorts of duties –
Air Raid Wardens, Special Constables, Rescue Workers, Firemen, Nurses
– giving a gentle hint there might be a war but everything was being done
to avert it. Meanwhile, we carried on as before, working and playing,
almost forgetting what might lie ahead until one day we heard a most
awful wailing sound coming from the direction of Diss. We could not
fathom the meaning of what this strange sound was until we heard the
next day they were trying out the air-raid sirens. This news brought us
back to reality. We thought they must know something as they wouldn't
go to all these lengths for nothing. Another year passed while the village
life carried on, hasty preparations were being carried out, air-raid shelters
were being made in all the cities, sand bags were being filled. Composers,
sensing a war was a distinct possibility, were writing songs to suit the
occasion. Soon we were playing 'Siegfried Line' and 'Run Rabbit Run',
etc.

Training for the civil defence went on and a new body of men was
formed to protect our island; they were called Local Defence Volunteers,
later to be known as the Home Guard. We really knew then that things
were getting serious and we wondered what would become of our band. If
we were called up, would we ever see each other again? These thoughts
went through my mind as I carried on with my daily work; here was I just
an ordinary young village man about to follow my forefathers' footsteps
and fight another war! It did not bear thinking about and the more I
thought the worse I felt and although everyone tried to put on a brave
face, the depressing thoughts could not be shaken off. We still played
cricket and concerts were still arranged in the village but without the same
enthusiasm. To add to the rumours of war it so happened that at this time

the telegraph lines were being placed underground. This set the locals talking at their nightly 'mardle' (chat) and it was rumoured that the wires had been taken off the poles so that the 'Jerries' could not cut them if they invaded. All sorts of reasons were forthcoming but nobody thought this was simply another advancement in the telegraph system. The poles had to go with the coming of the very fine cables which could go underground with much more efficiency. Things were moving too fast for the older generation at that time to take in but, being of the next generation, I could accept these changes more readily although I must admit it all seemed like a dream world, looking back at the many changes I had witnessed in my life.

We even acquired our own 'Woolworths' in Diss whereas before we could only visit these exciting stores when in Great Yarmouth or Norwich. We thought we were being honoured when we first heard of this store coming to Diss, such was the childlike anticipation for anything new among the population at that time. Similarly, when Mr Stevens announced he was going to build a new cinema, we all got very excited, rich and poor alike. When at last it was built next to the old tin hut, there was a mad stampede for tickets for the first week's film, which was Jessie Matthews in 'Evergreen'. The cinema held 408 patrons; there would be two houses each night and every seat would be taken when the more popular films were shown, especially Laurel and Hardy as we country folk loved a good laugh. I can remember when 'Gone With the Wind', starring Clark Gable, was shown, it lasted four hours, allowing only one house each night, so it stayed in Diss for two weeks as it was so popular. Similarly, everyone wanted to see Snow White and the Seven Dwarfs.

Getting back to the seeming approach of war, things were certainly moving towards that end when the evacuees arrived from London to Diss Station, to be distributed to homes in the villages around Diss, looking wide-eyed and frightened at the prospect of what was in store for them. The villagers themselves were very apprehensive and suspicious of what they had let themselves in for by agreeing to take these children in. However, most of the children settled down to their life in the country and were sorry to leave when it was time for them to do so, having made new friends. Others found it hard to accept the country way of life and a few were naughty and sent home. All of them found it very strange to have to go to the toilet at the bottom of the garden, especially after dark, with all the leaves rustling and often a rat scurrying out of the way, and no flush and worst of all no lights, only what they carried, lantern or candle. Country life was definitely not what these children had expected, but with a few exceptions they adapted to this new life wholeheartedly. With all this activity around me I was not surprised when several practice blackouts were ordered. This meant lights had to be concealed from the air after a certain time and then on the fateful day when war was declared this became a reality and heavy fines were enforced on anybody showing a light after dark. To add to the certainty of war, a regiment of soldiers were stationed at Diss. They were mostly young, learning the trade, so to speak. Every night patrols and guards would be placed at various points around the town. Local people who ventured out after dark would be stopped and challenged by these young soldiers who would say 'Halt! Step forward and be recognized!' This frightened some of the more nervous residents but to some of us it became quite a game and we would go out and about on purpose to be challenged. The regiment stationed at Diss was the Royal Army Service Corps and they commandeered the Church Hall for their canteen and it was not long before some of us in uniform (be it only that of a Fireman) were allowed in to sample their food; quite a treat for us.

We decided to cease our band activities as it was obvious by now that there was no point in continuing with boys being called up. We were sure it would not be long before we followed suit and so it was decided to take on no more engagements. A sad day for us.

It was not long after that our age group began having medical examinations and I was instructed to attend for mine in Norwich. When asked what service I would prefer, I said 'The RASC' thinking I would be able to continue with my driving. How wrong I was, when at last I received my call up papers, I was instructed to take the train to Norwich to join the Norwich Fire Brigade. This was because of the training I had received in Diss. I had been married the year before and was living in one of the estate cottages and was receiving wages of one pound eighteen shillings per week. So imagine how I felt when, upon receiving my call-up to the City Brigade, I was told my wage would be three pounds ten shillings per week plus another fifteen shillings subsistence allowance. This represented quite a fortune to me and if it had not been the threat of the dreadful war which was now in progress I would have been excited at the prospect of being able to save money at last.

When Sir Edward heard I had received my call-up and was told how much I would be earning, he asked 'Whatever are you going to do with all that money?' He disappeared into the Hall to ponder on the changing ways of life. As for myself, I suddenly realized I would be receiving more than the Head Gardener. I could not believe it! thirty-eight shillings per week might seem low, but it was the going rate at that time for land workers.

The Diss Firemen on duty the day World War II was declared. Back L to R:
T Wells; Author; C Kedge. Front L to R: A Ellinor; G Rice (Leading Fireman).

The months preceding my actual leaving for Norwich were punctuated with small brushes with what the war was all about, in attending many fires caused by incendiary bombs in the Diss area. The worst incident was when a lone bomber was returning home to Germany in the early hours on 15 September, 1941, and it scored a direct hit with a bomb on Roydon Hall, killing one of the maids and injuring another. I attended this incident and it was the first time war was really brought home to me in all its horror. A sight implanted on my memory forever.

Chapter 40

I Head Into the Unknown

The day finally arrived when I had to depart along with two other Diss Firemen, namely Frank Hines and Graham Norman, for duty at the Head-quarters of the City Fire Brigade in Norwich. Our train fare had been provided and we duly arrived at the appointed time with several others from other towns and villages all over Norfolk. After being accepted, we were billeted to different addresses in the City. Frank Hines and myself found ourselves in Queens Road at the home of an elderly couple. We soon settled in and reported for duty the next day, when we were more or less told the reason for us being drafted into Norwich. It was to reinforce the City Brigade in case of air raids which could be expected at any time. Intensive training would begin at once in rescue work and how to evacuate the hospitals. This we did with great care and thought. The West Norwich Hospital was the one we practised on. This presented quite a task as at that time ninety per cent of the patients were elderly and had to be comforted before strapping them to a stretcher and lowering them from the windows to the ground. It must have been a fearful experience for them, swinging in the air, lying on a stretcher. However, this exercise proved invaluable as this hospital received a direct hit in a raid at a later date but very few lives were lost due to the skill of the rescue services and the staff.

During the next few months, training went on at an ever-increasing pace. My worst moments were when we had to have a real gas training session. This consisted of a brick construction fifteen feet square with just a door and no windows. Our instructor would place a canister of gas inside, and a dummy, and we would then each in turn have to crawl in and identify the type of gas used by slightly lifting the side of our respirator, taking a small sniff and then bring out the body by feeling for it in complete darkness. Quite an eerie experience, although we knew it was only a dummy. On emerging from the chamber we had to say what gas was being used – the most dangerous one was Mustard gas and when taking a sniff we were told to be very brief owing to the dangerous effects this could have if not treated with extreme care. Fortunately, the Home Office stopped training using real gas as it was deemed highly unlikely we would have to contend with it on a major scale. We then had to train hard on the use of ladders. The most terrifying was the vertical wall, carrying your ladders with you. Each ladder was nine foot long with two three-foot hooks projecting from one end. This you would hook into the first-floor window, then put the second ladder on your shoulders and scale the first ladder, then sit on the window sill with one leg hanging out. Then the exercise would be repeated with your second ladder by hooking it onto the window sill above, and so on, all the way to the top of the building – quite an unnerving experience especially for we young men raw from the country. When we had a turntable ladder we would proceed to the highest building at the fire station and be left on the flat roof to be rescued by this ladder, which extended to 100 feet. A rope would be passed through a pulley at the top of the ladder to the ground through a series of worm gear. Our officer would fasten the rope around each one of us in turn, the ladder would then lift, taking us with it, and we would be swinging in the air before being lowered to the ground 100 feet below. Another experience taking me further away from the quiet days of village life. I again wondered why all this was happening. Training went on apace, we had to learn all the sources of water throughout the city and the methods of dealing with the evacuation from large buildings. This was quite a job as in an emergency every one of us had to know exactly where everything was and how to deal with any situation.

We were on strict rations and would join in a queue just to see what was on offer at the other end of it. Often it would be fruit or something not very important but queue we did, because everyone else did; it became quite a habit. Every morning for breakfast we had rolled sausage meat in flour at our lodgings and this went on for six months without a change. We got so sick of it that we pretended to eat but secretly dropped it into a paper bag between our knees. We then went for a walk after breakfast so we could dispose of it in the nearest bin. We would then queue at the cake shop for whatever they had. Many and varied were the stories about where you could get this or get that. The black market was in evidence as in other cities although I never did get involved in it. I knew what was going on but pretended I didn't. Although I was green and from the country, I soon realized it was better to remain that way.

I attended many small fires in the city and learned a lot about the mysteries of war, inasmuch as to where some commodities were being stored in case of emergency. We discovered one house crammed full of razor blades, thousands of packets. We learned they were for the troops. Another time, when a church was on fire, we discovered it to be full of sugar, thousands of tons packed from floor to ceiling.

The fire service engines and crews were spread out all over the city so as not to be in one place, in case of a direct hit. There were about six crews stationed at different places, all controlled from the main city station at Bethel Street, this was in turn controlled from the Fire Force Headquarters at Hethersett. I was stationed at Bethel Street and Hall Road alternately. Things seemed to be quiet in the world of war preparation, apart from watching the balloons going up and down at regular intervals. The city was ringed with these to deter low flying aircraft. The siren often sounded and the odd enemy plane appeared near the city. We had to keep guard all night from the various stations and also two of us had to watch the city from the City Hall clock tower. It could be very eerie up there if alone. We were connected by telephone to Headquarters and had to inform them if fires were seen. We could even see the fires from the steam train engines when the drivers opened the fire doors to put some coal on.

There is always a daredevil among a large body of men and we had such a person at our station. While on duty on the tower one night I heard a voice cry 'I done it! I done it!' coming from the room we had up there. I asked 'Done what?'

'Why, I have just walked on the outside of the guard rails on the nine-inch cement surround, right round the tower. I have always wanted to do that' was the reply. I said 'You must be crazy, what if you had slipped? It's 150 feet down there.' He turned a bit pale as if the truth of the possible circumstances had just sunk in, and then said 'Oh, well, it's done, don't tell'.

The war brought me the chance to learn jobs I never dreamed I could do. For instance, on our off-duty days in Norwich we had to help where needed most. I found myself working part-time in a heavy machine shop in Riverside Road where Churchill tanks were being made, amongst other steel products for the war, such as steel containers for the invasion of Europe. I had quite a simple job, putting on the handles by rivets. It was very boring but the noise in the shop from the other workers quite deafened me and I couldn't hear a thing at night when leaving the factory so I had to stop this little sideline as I had to have good hearing to drive a fire engine.

I was then asked to help at the Theatre Royal, as a scene shifter. I was very confused at first with all the signs painted on the floor and on the back of each stage prop, such as 'O.P.' which meant Opposite Prompt, and the other side which was marked 'Prompt Side'. I really enjoyed this work, especially during the pantomime season. We often had to remain on stage during a scene, holding up some of the scenery and although we were well concealed behind the scenery, it was quite an ordeal to remain still for ten minutes or longer and particularly difficult to keep a straight face at some of the jokes being told. The performers did not like us to stare at them from such close quarters and in fact some of them could get quite shirty over the least little setback.

I well remember an incident when there was a circus on stage. Imagine the scene: there was a ring of horses standing quietly round this large stage, waiting to perform their act after the chorus girls who were doing their dancing routine in front of the main curtain which, of course, was down. The first night these girls were dancing backwards and forwards, throwing their legs up to the music with their fixed smiles which all dancers have, when one of the horses decided to relieve itself on the other side of the curtain. It happened at the point where there was a gap in the middle of the curtains and as the girls danced past they were drenched with urine and steam. They carried on until the dance finished but then I heard the most foul language I have ever heard from girls. They screamed and shouted, swore and told the producer that if those *** horses were there at the next performance he could get someone else to do the dance. They would *** off. They were not there to be *** on and so it went on. They pushed past me, looking like demons instead of the pretty girls the audience thought they were. After that there was much confusion for the rest of the night. But the show went on, as did many more, including 'The Desert Song' which I was privileged to see. The war did have its lighter moments!

Chapter 41

Music To My Ears

Imagine my surprise one day when, looking at the notice-board in the station, I saw a notice saying the forming of a Fire Service Dance Band was contemplated and would musicians please put down their names. Reg Read would be the leader, auditions would take place as soon as there were enough names. I lost no time in adding my name to the list, although at that time I had no idea who the others were or what each one could play or what level of playing ability was expected. I knew I was only a village boy who had played the drums in a small village band and had no experience of playing with a professional band. However, I thought this is a chance I must take, so I put the war thoughts in the background and began to wonder would I be good enough, if chosen? After a week a list was pinned up with four names, mine included, for the drummer's vacancy. I had already bought another set of drums from a fellow fireman who was hard up and let me have them at a reasonable price. I prepared myself for the trial practice with the drummer from the Samson & Hercules Ballroom band as judge. Much to my surprise I was chosen as drummer for the newly formed band. I was not a fancy drummer but was considered all right, so I was told. A whole new era then opened up for me which was to last while I was stationed in Norwich. We not only formed a band, but a concert party as well, with CO Bush in charge. We played all over the County for wartime charities and all sorts of benevolent funds. Also music while they worked in some factories and a lot of children's parties. My greatest moment was when we played on the massive Regent Cinema stage at the interval between films which were again for the war effort. I shall never forget the moment sitting behind those huge curtains, waiting for our turn to play 'I don't want to set the world on fire' in front of a packed house, with the spotlights on us. Even at that moment in my life my mind went back to those happy childhood days in the harvest fields, watching the loads of corn brushing through the hedges at the gateways on their way home to the farm. The smell of the horses and the song of the birds, in only a few seconds all this passed before my eyes until I was jolted back to reality with the sound of that large number of people clapping as we appeared. Again, I thought how could I, a country boy, be lucky enough to experience this? I was thankful.

Although the band enjoyed all these diversions, we still had to fulfil our duties as firemen. Most of our outside engagements were at night, during the day we trained with the others as usual and when we arrived home, whatever the hour, we had to take the next turn of guard duty, however tired we were, so it was not all roses.

I remember while on guard duty at the Central Station I had an experience which was quite unnerving. We had previously been told to beware of German paratroopers as some had been reported in various places in the country. This particular night I was on guard when at about 1 a.m. I heard a shuffling sound with chains tinkling and a figure loomed up out of the

The National Fire Service Band and Concert Party, Norwich, 1942. Author at top back right.

darkness in airman's clothes. On my challenge he spoke in a foreign language. I thought 'A Jerry!' I pretended I wanted to help him and gently escorted him to the Police station just around the corner where an armed policeman took over and they disappeared into the Police station. It was not until the following morning that I learned he was a Polish airman who had been shot down and was lost.

Chapter 42

Norwich Can Take It

Just for the record, there were 619 firemen in Norwich at this time. Although I mention this, I am not writing this book to prove facts, just to relate how the world looked through my eyes and how my innermost feelings reacted to what I saw and experienced as time went by.

The first raid on Norwich came on 27 April 1942. I was in my lodgings when the sirens went, followed almost at once by the drone of the offbeat German aeroplanes which dropped thousands of incendiaries followed by the high explosives, hundreds of them. I waited until the worst of the raid was over before venturing through the streets to the fire station, where I was ordered to Oak Street as driver of one of the appliances. On reaching our destination there was little we could do as all water mains were cut off. The stench was awful. Then there was that terrible noise of the timber beams as they tore themselves apart, crashing down with the weight of the buildings above. The cries of the children, the sound of ambulance bells, the smell of cordite hung in the air, and we firemen chasing for water and helping where we could. One Norwich resident said he thought the world had come to an end. Amidst all this, the Salvation Army, Church Army vans and YMCA vans all worked in relays from the rest centres, providing steaming hot cups of soup and tea to all the units of rescue and firemen wherever they could be found amidst all the confusion. It was on this night that the Norwich Hippodrome Theatre received a direct hit. Only hours before I had attended a performance there and watched the performing seal with great interest. Sadly, his trainer was killed – he was living in a trailer at the rear of the building – but the seal survived. I felt very sad at hearing this, but there were so many more such incidents in the days ahead, that one got hardened to it, if 'hardened' is the right word. Anyway, we learned to accept what Hitler might throw at us, but however brave one appeared to look and act, the truth was we were all scared but realized we had to stick it out; there was nowhere else to go.

The next big raid happened two nights later. This time it was a fire raid; thousands of incendiaries rained down and then several explosions. This time we were told to wait until the worst was over before going onto the streets, they said a live fireman was better than the risk of getting killed.

The Author aged 29.

Anyway when everything was falling around you it is impossible to concentrate, it was bad enough when the all clear sounded. Clambering over the twisted metal and girders, dragging hoses, it was very tiring work. We did this non-stop for two days and nights until we were relieved by firemen from London.

We were told to have twenty four hours rest, so Frank and I decided to walk to Earlham Park where it was nice and quiet, to get a few hours undisturbed sleep. In the distance we saw a large marquee and thinking this would offer us a nice windbreak we lay down, leaning against it and were soon fast asleep.

We slept for four hours and on waking I said to Frank 'What is this tent doing in this lonely part of the park in the middle of a war?' Frank said he didn't know and suggested we look inside. We lifted up the tent from the bottom and got the shock of our lives. It was full of the dead bodies from the raids, all laid out in neat rows. We dropped the tent wall back, jumped up and made a hasty retreat. I don't think our sleep did us much good!

At a later date a land mine dropped at the back of Gertrude Road. An officer and myself were sent there to see if there were any casualties. There were none, but the nature of the crater astounded us. It was 100 yards across and 60 feet deep. It reached up to some council houses, at one of which an air raid shelter was suspended over the huge crater. Inside was a small child, still asleep.

Another incident was when we were called to St Giles where a bomb had dropped in the middle of a brewery yard. Two lorries were burnt out but a third had been lifted onto the roof of the building, standing on its wheels with the tyres blown off. On the wall below was a rabbit hutch, in which a rabbit sat eating a cabbage leaf as if nothing had happened, while all around was death and destruction.

There were many more amazing stories to tell of the freak things which happened, such as the bomb which dropped in London Street, taking out every alternate window, leaving the others intact. Another astounding event which I witnessed.

One of my most uncanny experiences was the night I was on duty at the Hall Road station when the siren sounded, followed at once by the drone of enemy aircraft which seemed to hover overhead and then depart on its return journey. I wondered why the sudden return but I did not have long to wonder. Suddenly the dark night turned into brilliant light from the spectacular illumination of the parachute flares dropped by the plane which had just departed. I have never witnessed anything like it; every nook and cranny was illuminated – there were no shadows. I myself stood out like a statue, throwing no shadow, it was most uncanny. I suddenly realized they were going to bomb that area. After sounding the alarm, we were ordered to hastily take the fire appliances away from the station and disperse them at various points in case of a direct hit. Fortunately, on this occasion, the wind drifted the flares away from our area into the country where little damage was caused by the ensuing raid.

One night there was a violent thunderstorm and our crew were ordered to King's Lynn to reinforce the local brigade. I was the driver and a more nightmare drive would be hard to imagine. The rain was torrential, making it almost impossible to see as we had only blackout lights on the fire engine to see by. The thunder was deafening and the lightning was almost blue. We were forced to stop a while and we could hear the lightning snap, it was so close and sharp. On returning to Norwich we were confronted with wires strung across the road, resulting from the barrage balloons being struck by lightning. These were a double hazard due to the presence of high tension electric cables across which the wires trailed. We arrived back at the station completely exhausted, not through fighting fires but from the nightmare journey we had endured.

On another occasion we were called to retrieve some mystery objects from the roof of the Norwich Hospital. These were metal canisters with a small propeller attached and a small parachute connected to a seemingly endless wire, which carried them every thirty yards or so. The wire trailed over all the roof, including the nurses' home across the road. We had a very difficult job retrieving these canisters and getting them down to the fire engine on which we were placing them, wondering all the time what they were, having never experienced anything like these before. We had collected about a dozen, when all of a sudden a voice shouted 'Leave them alone. It's not your department, it's a job for the Army.' The voice came from an officer of the Bomb Disposal Department, who in no uncertain terms let us know who was in charge. We quickly returned to the ground and unloaded our engine of its mystery load and, with our tails between our legs, beat a hasty retreat to the station. We were informed later that the objects we had collected were very dangerous and could have exploded at any time with a devastating effect. They were part of a secret weapon devised to be dropped from an aeroplane flying higher than the bombers below when a raid was imminent. The idea was that this long wire would parachute down amongst the planes and get tangled up in their propellers and either bring down the planes or the canisters would explode resulting in the same effect. Anyway, it was top secret and we were glad we had escaped just with a telling off.

Another narrow escape was at a later date when the Americans were daylight bombing. It was 8.30 a.m. when, as usual at that time, the American bombers were forming high in the sky into the large formations some hundreds strong, preparing for their journey into enemy territory. Sometimes two planes would collide, spinning to the ground with their crew of ten and the load of high explosives. This happened on several occasions during my time with the fire service and the planes would land about ten miles apart, killing all the crew, leaving us to attend and extinguish the flames where possible. It always upset me to see this waste of young life, some of them were much younger than me. On this particular occasion we were called to a stricken plane some twelve miles into the country, it was in a field quite a long way from the road. We had to drive the full length of a meadow about a quarter of a mile long to reach the plane which was ablaze and quite destroyed. In it we saw the bodies of the crew, by now just a charred mass. Bombs were all over the place, several still in the plane, others scattered over a wide area. We were busy trying to damp the flames down with foam when all of a sudden a red jeep came tearing down the field with American bomb experts on board. They took one look at the nearest bomb and shouted to us 'Get the hell out of here, these are timed and will go up any minute now. The impact has set them going.' With that warning shout they reversed their jeep and made a hasty retreat to the road, we made a dash for our appliance and all scrambled aboard. I put my foot down and made for the road as fast as I could get up speed. The officer in charge said to me 'Straight back to Norwich, Talbot, sod the hose!' In our hurry to get away we had left several lengths of hose near the aeroplane. We had not travelled any more than a half mile down the road when crump! crump! crump! went the bombs as they exploded in quick succession. I think we nearly all fell off our machine with the shock of knowing what we had just escaped.

Although we were not exactly in the trenches in the war, we did have our moments of extreme danger. Like the night of the first big raid when one of our most well-liked officers was killed in Duke Street – C Officer Bussey. Another night an anti-personnel bomb fell near the turntable ladder, cutting the main elevator jack clean in half and just missing the fireman standing nearby. There were many other near misses in the city and many courageous stories could be told, enough to fill several volumes. I have only described what I actually took part in, as is the true intention of my book, presenting part of my life's journey and how I reacted to the many changes experienced.

Chapter 43

Hitler Repaid With Interest

After a spate of bombing by the enemy, each visit being less intense, raids petered out into the odd single plane venturing near the city until there were no more instances in our area but the rest of the country was being visited. Consequently, we were on constant standby for reinforcing distant brigades. We had only six minutes to answer a regional call. We did travel to Ipswich one night on the way to London which was being heavily bombed, but were recalled the next day, so I did not experience working in London as we at first feared.

By now we were listening to a different sound in the early evening. The sound of hundreds of our mighty bombers passing overhead on their way to Germany. The air vibrated with the sound of the heavily laden Lancasters and the sky seemed full of them – spaced about 400 yards apart as far as the eye could see. For over an hour this mighty armada of planes kept coming and when the final drone of their engines faded, we could not help but feel a great sense of pride and thankfulness that at long last we were able to hit back and repay Hitler for some of the horrors he had unleashed on the world. It was the day after we first experienced the thrill of watching the largest number of planes on their way that we were told this was the first of a thousand-bomber raid, there were many such raids to follow.

It was not long before there was talk of a second front and we were told we must be prepared to follow any such landings on the continent to help quell the many fires which were expected if the enemy decided on a 'scorched earth' policy. Also the whole distribution of the Fire Service would have to be reorganized. Daylight raids were to be stepped up by the Americans, too, to give support to ground troops when any landings took place. Consequently many empty large houses were commandeered for servicemen. One such building was 'The Paddocks' at Scole, quite close to my home at Thelveton. It was to be occupied by a contingent of firemen from London and a person was required with local knowledge if possible (as there were no signposts) to look after the food and be a Mess Manager. 'This is my chance to get back to the area I know and love so well,' I thought. So I put in my request in writing and to my joy I was selected for the post. My only sadness at leaving Norwich was saying goodbye to the many friends I had made, especially Ethel and William, the landlady and her husband, who was a leading fireman with me. But it was not exactly goodbye as we have kept in touch all these last fifty years and are still meeting in our old age and enjoy a day out together. The other love it was sad to leave was the Fire Service Band – it carried on with a fresh drummer for quite some time. Sadly some of the bandsmen have passed on, as have most of the men I did service with, but I am getting ahead of myself in my enthusiasm to relate the changes and opportunities which came my way.

I arrived at 'The Paddocks' full of apprehension at what my future held in this new venture. I had volunteered for the job and had had a crash course on mess managing with the officer in charge of catering at Norwich. I was told I would be allowed two shillings a day per person for food which had to include breakfast, lunch and evening meal. Sounds impossible? I thought so at first, but when I got down to working my sums out I found it could be done. Remember we were on strict rationing and allowed only an ounce of this and an ounce of that. The bulk of the food was made up of dried egg powder which was very good and went a long way. Potatoes were five shillings (25p) a hundredweight and were easily obtainable from local farmers and would make up a large portion of the main meals. Ducks' eggs were a shilling each if you could get them, but as I was on my home ground so to speak I was able to obtain a fair supply.

Although I was in charge of the catering, I was still a driver for the fire appliance and attended many incidents, chiefly plane crashes. Several were caused by two American planes colliding when getting into formation ready for leaving. It always upset me to attend these as there were ten young airmen to be accounted for from each plane and their bodies were sometimes to be found scattered about in gardens and the fields nearby, but mostly were still in the plane, burned beyond recognition. A terrible thing this war – here was I, almost in the same fields as I had played in as a child hunting rabbits at harvest time and generally helping to get the harvest in, enjoying every minute of those wonderful years, and now reaping the harvest of Hitler. Little did I think in those golden years that I, as a village boy, would one day witness such sights as I now had to contend with in the same fields. I am glad that as a youngster I could not foresee the sorrow that war was to bring but at the same time I am glad that as an adult I was able to render some small contribution to clearing up the aftermath of Hitler's bombers. I was only one of thousands in that great struggle and there was growing tension as D Day drew nearer, date as yet unknown. We were told to prepare to follow troops into Europe so we were always in a nervous state of readiness. We were allowed 12 minutes to pack our gear, blankets etc., in the event of a call to the place of embarkation.

As the bombing by the Americans and British intensified, more fires and crashes occurred so we were kept very busy. But it was not all work in the evening and when possible we would visit the local pubs. Beer was in short supply but one of our number who had worked in a brewery before being called up had a perpetual thirst. He said he used to drink a pailful of beer before breakfast – the wooden pails they used in the brewery. When allowed out, he would make for the pub as fast as he could and by the time any of the rest of us got there he had already consumed twelve pints of beer. By the time the night was over, he could and would sink up to thirty pints. When we arrived back at the Paddocks we would all make sure we went to the toilet before 'Diddy' got there and we would lay in bed listening to him relieving himself before retiring. This would often take a good five minutes but he never got up again all night; a lovely and remarkable man. On one occasion we were all called on parade to be informed we were to get a rise in pay which would be back-dated three months. The officer in charge at this point said 'Ah! I can see Diddy is busy working out how many extra pints he will get!' Such diversions helped to make life just that little more humane during the horrors of war.

We had little protection when attending a blazing plane, with bullets flying in every direction and we were told to grab a dustbin lid from someone's house if possible and hold this in front of us as a shield. When approaching a plane I don't think these would have stopped many of the bullets had we encountered some. Fortunately, of all the crashes we dealt with nothing more than minor burns were ever experienced.

One morning a plane crashed on take-off from the nearby airfield. It landed quite close to the road in a field and most of the crew escaped or were accounted for. One crew member was trapped by his legs and was screaming with fear as although the plane had not caught fire it was in danger of doing so at any time. The airman knew this, hence his cries for help. I was one of the first ones to arrive and felt totally helpless looking up at this large plane (a Flying Fortress) knowing I dare not interfere with trying to release him as we were so close to the air base from where help would arrive at any minute. When help did arrive, there was a fire tender, ambulance, rescue vehicles and an array of men. The Americans certainly looked after their personnel, which the following ending of this story will particularly illustrate. As soon as they arrived, to my amazement instead of trying to release the airman at once, the first thing they did was light a cigarette and give it to him, then produce a comic paper for him to read while they carried out the difficult job of cutting him loose. He was actually laughing at the things he was reading although I think he must have still been panic-stricken.

On another occasion when two planes collided, one came down quite near us and we were asked to attend in case of fire. All the airmen with the exception of one were dead in the plane. The one airman who had escaped was dangling from his parachute in a tree, screaming. He was only a very young man. It was not long before a jeep arrived with two 'Snowdrops' on board (American Police, so called because of their white hats). After releasing the screaming airman from the tree, they bundled him into the jeep and, without further ado left the scene for a hurried return to their base where, I was told, another plane would be waiting into which he would be forced, still screaming with fear, to be taken up at once so as to cure him of the dread of flying again. I was told that if they did not do this he would have never flown again.

There were many incidents such as this during the remainder of our stay at the Paddocks and it would take many pages to record all the acts of courage I witnessed. One such act was the great armada flying over our headquarters to the Arnheim invasion. There were great numbers of planes, towing their gliders and hours later we saw those same planes returning, minus their gliders, having, as someone said, 'Dumped their human loads on some foreign land to add to the waste of lives in this war.' One plane I shall always remember returned with a soldier still dangling in his parachute, this having been caught up on the plane somewhere. He would have been dead by the time he had travelled all those miles home. I cannot forget that sight of one who went and returned and died without fighting. Even after fifty-odd years I still shudder at that thought. Some things do remain in my memory for ever!!

The D Day invasion came early in June as was expected. We were not required to land with the troops, much to our relief, as the 'scorched earth' policy did not take place due to the rapid advance of the Allies. The Scole Paddocks were closed as a fire station and I was sent to Beccles in the same capacity as Mess Manager. This was at the time of the 'Doodlebug', Hitler's secret weapon, and I often heard them going over. They had a very frightening sound – like a noisy tractor – and we pretended not to be nervous but it was always a relief when the sound died away in the distance and had not cut out overhead as these were terrible weapons whey they dropped from the sky, causing much damage and death.

After a while a full-time fire station was formed in Diss and I was transferred there due to my local knowledge and I attended many more aeroplane incidents. By this time the war was chiefly in the Far East, although there was still plenty of activity going on as the battle was closing in on Berlin. We had one serious incident while I was stationed at Diss – a plane crashed into the middle of the bomb storage dump at Thorpe Abbotts airfield. We were called to the scene, knowing full well the danger which lay ahead. If the dump had blown up we would have been blown to kingdom come, along with half the camp personnel. It was with these thoughts raging in my head that I drove the engine as fast as I could towards the camp, not feeling too good, I can tell you. As we neared the camp a most amazing sight greeted us. Americans were streaming from the camp, coming across the fields and down the road in large numbers to escape the almost certain death had they stayed and the dump had exploded. Some of them managed to stop their headlong flight and direct us to the danger area where black smoke was pouring into the sky some quarter-mile further on. We hurried on, not knowing what to expect. When we arrived and got within 300 yards of the dump we were told to stop by the Military Police who were on duty, seemingly on an empty road. Much to our relief we were informed our service would not be required as this was a military detail and we should not have been called out in the first place. They would deal with it and as a little appreciation we were invited to stay for lunch. Well, having been on rations so long, the sight of so much food in the Mess Hall had a lasting impression. Steaks were there seemingly by the hundred and fruit dessert in churns which the Americans liked to mix with their meat. We had such a feast that it was never to be forgotten. It certainly made up for the frightening experience on the journey there. The bomb dump did not go up as the plane burnt itself out without setting the bombs off.

Chapter 44

The War Ends and I Return to Civvy Street

As the war seemed to be nearing its end, I began to seriously think about what I wanted to do when it was all over. Fate seemed to take a hand when I saw an advertisement in our local paper regarding a cottage which was for sale by auction. I spoke to my wife about it who seemed to like the idea of us buying a house of our own. 'But where is the money coming from?' she asked. I said we could borrow it from a Building Society and wrote to one. I was told I could bid for the cottage and go up to seven hundred pounds. I was really excited and thought I stood a very good chance as houses were not selling very well in war time due to the risk of them being bombed. The day of the auction arrived. I had permission from my Officer to attend and was very nervous as this was the first time I had attempted anything like this. An ordinary working man buying a house was an unheard thing and probably frowned upon by some of the employers in the area. However, a change was coming, I could somehow feel it in my bones, and was urged by some inner being to go ahead. I felt better thinking these things and started my bidding with a new zest. I got as far as my limit of seven hundred pounds and much to my disappointment it went another fifty pounds before being knocked down to a Colonel and Mrs Twiss. However, I was not finished yet. I decided to wait to see who these people were, so after the room was cleared I sat there watching Col. and Mrs Twiss complete the formalities with the Solicitors. I then plucked up courage and, touching my cap, I said 'Excuse me Madam, I hope you won't think me rude by asking, have you bought the cottage for anyone or are you going to let it?' The lady replied 'I have just bought a big house in the next village of Roydon, it has a large garden and I have bought this cottage for a gardener. I shall want one as soon as this war is over.' I nearly fell over in my excitement to explain to her that I was a gardener and would be looking for a job after the war as I wanted to branch out on my own, that was why I was trying to buy the cottage. It was the lady's turn to feel surprised and unable to contain her excitement at what I had told her. She said 'What a coincidence, us both meeting here in these circumstances, you're wanting a cottage and a job, me wanting a gardener. It is too good to be true. Yes, subject to your references being in order, which I am sure they are, and you liking the garden, the job's yours.' I am sure fate was working for us.

I lost no time in conveying the good news to my wife, who was elated at the prospect. I then had to inform my officer my day had not been wasted. He replied by saying 'Now you had better tell Hitler to give up so you can start your new life. Anyway I am very pleased for you and hope this lot will soon be over. It shouldn't be long now.' As it happened, shortly afterwards the bomb which ended the war gave me the chance to begin my new way of life. I felt very strange at first, putting on working clothes and getting back on my bicycle again, and as I peddled along I began to worry if I had done the right thing. But then I thought I had got to take the plunge and if I didn't help myself and my family, no one else would. My greatest problem would be making my own decisions and not relying on the head gardener to give me orders, as I had been used to for my previous eleven years at the Hall.

When I arrived, the first thing I had to do was get acquainted with the woman whose job I was taking. She had carried on the best way she could and had made a very good job of it, creating a new lawn which was named after her and was always known as Mrs Greenwood's Lawn. I began by edging all the lawns as I think if the lawn edges are cut and tidy the whole place looks cared for. I could see all sorts of jobs needed doing and found it very hard to do them in the right order. It also took a long time for me to assume control and authority. I started to ask Mrs Twiss questions about this and that and she soon made it quite clear I was there to make my own decisions and she had absolute trust in my judgement. This made me feel important but I never let that feeling get the better of me. After a week or two, Mrs Greenwood left, and I had to take on fresh duties which she had been doing, such as chopping sticks and looking after the boiler for the house, looking after the car and cleaning boots and shoes. The pride and joy of 'The Friary' – the name of the house – was the herd of goats which took a lot of looking after. A girl had been employed for this job until she married when I had to learn to milk the animals, a job I had never visualized I would ever be asked to do. The goats were show animals and I had to take them to the 'Norfolk' and 'Suffolk' agricultural shows and stay the night, sleeping the best way I could. I chose to sleep in with the cowmen who were from the Hall where I used to work, while Mrs Twiss slept on a put-U-up with her goats. Yes, I was certainly getting a fair bit of variety in my life and more was to come.

The Friary where I now worked was a place after my own heart. In the middle of the country, surrounded by trees and ponds with all their wild-life, and plenty of birds singing around the whole area, which compensated me for all the years I had missed these sounds. They had now returned and served as a reminder of my happy boyhood days when these conditions were common to all. Memories often came flooding back to me. I had strolled along the many footpaths by the miles of huge hedges full of birds and their nests with their young poking their heads up for food, smelt the new-mown hay and heard the sound of men shouting from some distant farm. There were no tractors or cars in my childhood memories, only the occasional steam engine which, as I have said before, was music to my ears. After these thoughts came the reality of the present. Here was I thinking of the past when I had plenty of responsibilities for the present. Although I was now working full-time, I was still attached to the fire brigade and was called out on many occasions. As time went on, it became apparent it was wrong for me to neglect my work which involved animals for the sake of continuing as a fireman. So, reluctantly I resigned from the brigade and concentrated on my job. This was getting more complicated and interesting as time went on. Mrs Twiss came to me one day saying 'Talbot, I don't want to frighten you off, but I have been doing a lot of planning for the future which I am afraid involves you.'

Chapter 45

The Plans are Carried Out

'If it's to do with the garden, I don't expect I shall get frightened,' I told Mrs Twiss. 'Splendid,' she said. 'I will tell you what I have in mind. I eventually want this to be a show garden, it will involve you in a lot of hard work and it won't be achieved at once but will take a year or two. First of all I want a brick wall across the centre of the vegetable plot, with a gate in the middle, this will look silly at first but it is going to lead to the sunken garden I have in mind which is now the potato patch. This, in turn, will lead to a new lawn I want you to make. The vegetable patch will be turned into a massed flower display leading down to the pond, which will be surrounded by another raised display of dahlias. Next to that I would like a phlox garden which will bring us back to the loggia (summer house). To the west of that the entire garden of about a quarter of an acre will be made into a lawn surrounded by a snake-shaped garden backed by a chestnut fence. Well? What do you think of the prospect of carrying out this plan I have devised, Talbot?' With a flourish, she produced a large plan which she proudly displayed. I was taken aback to say the least but being young (in my thirties) I wholeheartedly agreed with the plan and said I would do my best to get it done in the shortest possible time.

The first thing I arranged was for a builder to pay us a visit for an estimate. In those days a builder was seldom asked to price a small job. They were paid at the end of the time it took with no questions asked, usually £5 or £6 per day maximum plus materials used. The work was completed within the next few weeks. I was then able to start digging out the sunken garden which was adjacent to the wall. This took me about two months to do as I had to fit it in between my many other gardening jobs, besides looking after the animals and poultry. I had the garden as it was to keep right. At this time 'Redgrave Hall' was to be sold by auction, bit by

144

bit, starting with the front door, then the floors, panels, all fittings, carved ceilings etc. Quite a massive undertaking; the hall was so big it took several days to sell all of it. I was asked by my employer to attend on her behalf to bid for the floor of the servants' hall, being all large paving stones three feet by two feet each, also another floor to match. Some 150 paving stones in all, these were to be used for the floor of the sunken garden I had just finished digging. I was entrusted with a signed blank cheque to pay for these at the sale. This gesture by my employer proved the trust and understanding we had for each other, we were working together as a team, rather than as an employer and servant. We both wanted the garden to look special and as each fresh improvement developed we were both visibly pleased with our achievements.

After purchasing the slabs, I had to arrange with our friendly builder, George Rackham, for the loan of his lorry and a man to fetch them home. This took several days and journeys on his small lorry. It was quite hard work, prising these slabs which had been down hundreds of years, then getting them out of the hall was another problem. As the windows had been removed by another buyer, we found it easiest to get the slabs through the window space rather than carry them down the long corridors of the mansion. It is a sad sight to see these wonderful old buildings being ripped apart. The man we took with us for an extra pair of hands was so upset and frightened at being in this great empty house he kept pleading with us not to leave him in there.

'I will get lost,' he said. 'Let's get out of here as quickly as we can.' I felt sorry for him, he was aged and this place had a profound effect on him. I must admit it did feel eerie.

I then had the job of putting all these slabs down over the next few months. I had to wheelbarrow them quite a distance in the garden, one at a time, they were so heavy, but I managed it. The effect was quite startling after seeing the plain ground for so long, then to see this new paved area with its flower beds and the raised beds all round. My employer was more than elated at what we had achieved so far and promptly invited a lot of her friends round to see it. They, too, were astounded at what had taken place in the short time since I arrived. I hasten to add that all this could not have been attempted but for the enthusiasm of my employer and the way she had accepted me and made me feel one of the family. My wife was treated in exactly the same way and we both knew we had made the right decision in starting this new life.

The Friary was a nice compact property with a large orchard of over 100 apple trees, mostly Cox, which required a lot of attention and as time went on Mrs Twiss could see that with all the extra work I had to do it was time she found me extra help. She began making enquiries and was rewarded by having a man nearing retirement age apply, who as it turned out was just the man for the job, having worked on the land all his life and being an excellent gardener too. He was a good time-keeper and a glutton for work. He was one of the old school of workers who I mentioned earlier who took a pride in his work and I could not have wished for anyone better. He was one of the few men I have known who did not need a line when working in the kitchen garden; he would look up and down the plot, then strike off with his toe, making a mark for the crop to be sown in or planted and it would always be dead straight. Few can do this!

The gardens were now beginning to take shape and I could see in my mind's eye the finished result. This spurred me on and by the time another spring had arrived, my employer decided to throw the gardens open to the public when they were at their best. It was an instant success and the church funds benefited considerably from the venture from that time onwards. Several organizations took advantage of Mrs Twiss's kind invitation and staged many of their meetings in her grounds. Two of the organisations were the Blind, who had their own helpers and enjoyed the smell of the flowers, and the old people's home at Pulham, and there were

The Friary Gardens, Roydon.

many others. I thoroughly enjoyed preparing the ground for these events and would often be at work making the lawns look nice at the crack of dawn. My wife, with other helpers, would organize teas on the lawns, I borrowed a gramophone and fixed loudspeakers about the grounds and relayed music which I thought they would like. All in all this was quite a place to work! It was not all pleasure, as the many jobs had to be attended to as well as the jobs in the house, keeping the car clean, digging half an acre of the kitchen garden in the winter and spring, then keeping it clean all summer, clipping the yew hedges which were over ten feet tall, but now I had some help and work seemed a lot lighter.

Mrs Twiss hated the English winter so she always went abroad to escape the worst of the weather. Australia was her favourite place to cruise to, it was the six weeks on board ship she enjoyed the most. By the time she was able to make her first trip, she had suffered the loss of her husband, Colonel Twiss, hence her desire to leave the Friary during the dark winter months. It was her wish that my wife and I should move into the Friary during her absence to be caretakers of her property. The arrangement worked very well, I was on the spot for any eventualities. It was a bit strange living in the Friary, having heard all sorts of ghostly stories regarding the monks. The first year we were asked to do this I

The Paved Garden at The Friary, Roydon.

thought I would surprise Mrs Twiss before she returned and get the last piece of garden which she so badly wanted made into a lawn. It was a fairly big job, even for two of us, to turn the quarter of an acre vegetable plot into a lawn. The grass was to come from an adjoining meadow and had to be cut by hand which Charles, my helper, did. When he had filled the barrow, he would push it over 100 yards to a board we had put across the deep ditch. I would meet him there, then push it across the board into the garden. I then had to cross about 40 yards of lawn before reaching the ground I was going to cover. After all that endeavour, I found I only covered a piece of ground about four-feet square with each barrow load! Looking back at the huge expanse of garden yet to be covered it seemed an impossible task for just the two of us, but cover it we did, although it took us nearly five months and we were proud of it. Charlie moaned a bit: 'I am no lawn man,' he said. 'Give me a good old vegetable plot to dig, that's more in my line. You can't eat grass.' However, even he was surprised at the difference this made to the size of the garden, it looked huge with so much grass. Before Mrs Twiss went, she had bought another bit of wooded land merely to turn into a new vegetable garden, when we could clear it. So we started clearing this as fast as we could so as to get a crop on it that year. Contractor Bryant lived opposite the Friary and would bring his tractor over each afternoon and pull up the saplings and small trees which were growing freely on the land. When these cleared he ploughed up the half acre of land and we were in business again. Although it was April there was still time to get a fair variety of vegetables in, including a big patch of kale for the animals.

The great day arrived when Mrs Twiss would be returning. I could hardly contain myself at the thought of what her reaction would be at seeing the biggest part of her plan finished. When I met her at the station off the evening train, her first words were, as always, 'How are you and Mrs Talbot, and my angel?' (Her dog). I said 'Fine, how are you yourself Madam?' and she replied 'Longing to see my lovely garden again. I expect it is looking nice with all the spring flowers.' I told her 'It's looking better than ever, there's a good show of everything.' 'Splendid,' she said. 'I have had a wonderful break but I am glad to be home.' With that we journeyed home and I then had to devise a way of surprising her with what had been accomplished in her absence. So when we got back to the Friary and she had kissed her dog and greeted my wife on the step, she said 'Now Talbot, show me the garden.' I asked 'Will you do exactly as I say and ask no questions?' Laughing, she said 'Don't tell me you have blown up the potting shed?' but I just said 'Do you mind looking over into the meadow while you are walking and I will say when you can look the other way. It's not as dreadful as you imagine!' Well! When we got level with the great new expanse of lawn, all neatly cut and edged, which before was just black soil, I said 'You may look this way now but be prepared for a pleasant surprise.' I cannot explain the look Mrs Twiss gave me after she had inwardly digested all that we had done in her absence. The pleasure was written in her eyes and her silence said everything. Her moment of realization of what she now possessed, the fulfilment of her wildest dream. The garden was now complete in every detail and had been accomplished in record time. Her eyes said it all and we both knew that sort of emotion which can only be present when a dream is realized. I quietly disappeared to put the car away, leaving her to ponder on this latest development.

Mrs Twiss was a real lady, being thankful for everything she had. She would never pass a tramp on the road if she had room in her car – a true lady in every sense of the word.

By now I was well-known in the village and was soon friendly with everyone, especially the older generation of 'Roydonians' as they liked to call themselves and it was not long before I learned Roydon had a good sporting background. It was a pity that something was not done in that direction as there were many youngsters with so much spare time on their hands. From this and many other chats with the locals I came to the conclusion it was a football team they were hankering after. If only someone would start the ball rolling, they looked at me as if I could be the answer to their wishes. I thought 'Why not! I am a football fan myself and it would be an achievement if I could make something out of all this.' The idea was born and I called a public meeting in the village pavilion to test the views of the parishioners. The meeting was a huge success being chiefly attended by the young men of the village who sensed this could mean the opportunity they had all been waiting for.

Chapter 46

I Play Again and Roydon Turns 'Blue and White'

The meeting was attended by the local Parson who was a keen football fan and many views were put forward. As I had called the meeting, I was asked to fulfil the job of Secretary and I accepted. Then came the question of what ground we would be playing on. I had already approached the Squire of the village for the use of his meadow opposite his house, bordering the main Thetford Road, and he said we could use his ground if we kept the noise down! So I had scored my first victory for the new club even before it started, much to the surprise of most of those present as it was thought no one would ever be allowed on the ground, let alone play football on it.

That night twelve Vice Presidents were elected and I lost no time in contacting them by letter as money from their subscriptions was needed to back the new club. So after the meeting had ended I wrote to all twelve and posted each letter the same night so as to make sure everyone knew as quickly as possible. I then contracted for goal posts and nets, and enlisted the help of 'Wiggy' Edwards of Diss, who was groundsman at the Grammar School, to mark the pitch out for us. He was a great help and let me into a secret before we started marking. This was 'There is a minimum size and maximum size for a football pitch. As you have a large meadow, make yours the maximum size. As most of the village teams play on small pitches, you will have the advantage when you play at home.' There was a lot of wisdom in his judgement as few teams did very well on our large pitch. The first game we played in the league was away from home and we lost 8–1 but this was against an experienced team and we never lost so heavily again; in fact we went on to reach the final for the Cup in our first

Roydon Football Club – late 1940s.

year. I now found myself in demand every week, running the club. I was not only Secretary but also marked out the pitch for each home game, travelled with the team and then wrote to the local paper under the heading 'Blue and White' – our colours. My wife washed all the strips each week, while George Rodwell and his wife carried out similar duties for the reserve team which was even more successful than the first team in the league. We had an excellent trainer in Leonard Manning, a former winger of Diss Town Football Team and so the football teams were established as the result of my meetings with the locals.

I always found myself with plenty to do. 'Your own making' my wife used to say. However, I was bubbling over with energy and was a glutton for work. Not only did I have to help dig half an acre of vegetable garden for my employer, I also had a half acre of allotment for myself. In between this was the animals to attend to, chauffeur work, home work and numerous other duties.

In the midst of all this I was approached by a friend who was anxious to start a dance band and he asked if I would like to be their drummer. I so liked music that I agreed, much to my wife's doubts as to the wisdom of taking on so much. I purchased another set of drums and we started practising. We called ourselves 'The Keynotes' and accepted engagements at Country Clubs at first. However, it was not long before we ventured further afield, such as at the Officers' Mess at Honington. We only went out one night a week though, not like the old days of every night dances. Times had changed, there was not the same excitement and enthusiasm as we had when we were young and besides there were few new tunes which resembled anything of the old ones. I must point out I am not condemning all the new tunes, some of them were very catchy and on an equal par to any of the others ever written, but I suppose it is because when we first played these lovely old melodies we were young, an experience one can never recapture.

I was now fully settled in my new life after the war and was determined to prove my early training would repay my determination to succeed. I often thought of my school days, especially as the farmer who lived opposite my place of work let me help him at harvest time. I also often gave other local farmers a hand at threshing time, bringing back still more memories of my golden youth. One day one of the workers was having a drink of hot tea from his Thermos flask and in a flash I remembered that back in the 1920s the flask had not been invented and the novel way the farm labourers had of keeping their bottles of tea warm was to stick their bottles in a muck heap. It sounds awful but was very effective.

When I first started at the Friary my employer thought she would help me by applying for a German prisoner of war from the camp nearby. I did not like the idea at first, having to be alone with a German, but Mrs Twiss assured me he would be quite safe as only the trusted ones were allowed out to work on the farms and gardens. There would be a bus load of them leave the camp and one or more would be dropped off as required, the driver returning for them at the end of the day. The prisoner I had was called Carl and he could not speak English. I still felt uneasy but he seemed all right and we got on together. As a matter of fact I learned quite a lot from him and although the war was not mentioned he made it quite clear he was not in favour of fighting. One day, when planting potatoes, he pointed out in his broken English that it was a waste to plant a whole potato. It would be better to cut out all the shoots and plant them in boxes. Then when these were established they could be planted out in the open, thus leaving the potato itself to be eaten, with no waste. It made sense but when I did get round to trying this idea, I found it much too fiddly. Besides, we could not eat all the potatoes that had been cut, so I abandoned the idea, but it would work if one had the patience and time. I lost my prisoner after a few weeks when the camp of Germans were transferred elsewhere and replaced by Italians. One of the Italians came to work with me. My employer asked me to get him to scythe the orchard but I did not like the idea of him having such a dangerous tool as a scythe. However, I was again assured that the prisoner would be incapable of violence as those allowed out to help on the land were all Grade C and came from gentler walks of life. But I was told they were not to be left with any valuables nearby as they might take them. I found this warning to be true as, much to my disappointment, I lost my watch by leaving it in the pocket of my jacket, hanging on the tree near where the prisoner was working. I did not say anything as he had this lethal weapon, the scythe, with him. As the man used the 'rub' or 'hone' to sharpen it continually I did not want to take any chances. By the end of the week he had sharpened the scythe so much that only a few inches were left of what had been a brand new tool. He used to have his lunch with the cook in the house, while I cycled home the mile journey to Diss. He must have liked the cook, as I had the devil of a job to get him out of the house at 2 p.m. to start work again. I told Mrs Twiss I would rather manage on my own than have the responsibility of looking after him, so after only a few weeks I found myself alone again. It was at this point that my employer decided to get me a more permanent man, as previously recounted.

However, I had not quite finished with my experiences of prisoners of war as a large gang of them came and worked in the fields nearby, clearing out the ditches and thinning the hedges. This was a government scheme to help the farmers with their drainage. One such gang were working next to the Friary when they spotted our large orchard of ripe apples and it was not long before a large number of these were taken under the blouses of these men, leaving a trail of dropped apples through the hedge. I dare not approach them, so I telephoned the local police who sent the Inspector to have a word with their guards. The Inspector asked if the prisoners had seen me about. When I said 'No' as they had only just arrived, he replied 'Good, they won't know who reported them. If they did, they would probably seek revenge, so I should lay low out of sight while they are working here.' I made sure I heeded his words and kept well out of the way. I was thinking I might get stabbed in the back as these prisoners were not as gentle as others previously encountered. All went well and the prisoners departed after having burned the hedge trimmings from the hedges they had thinned. The remarkable thing we noticed after they had gone was the large amount of elder bushes left and not burned with the rest of the rubbish. We found out afterwards that they were not allowed to burn elder as they were very superstitious and thought they would be cursed if any was burned, so they left it.

The time seemed to pass very quickly now, everyone was happy and it was not long before Mrs Twiss was off to Australia again for the winter break. Before she departed she said 'When you move into the Friary this time, I am offering you the Bishop's room to occupy as this is self-contained and will be more convenient for you. This room was so called as it had been occupied by a Bishop Friend on several occasions. In mid-December we moved in; there were twin beds for my wife and I and a camp bed at the foot of our beds for our son Russell, who was just three years old. All went well for the first few nights until one night we were woken by the most fearful clatter. I switched on the bedside light, not knowing what to expect. Much to our horror, the fire irons, together with the large brass fender, were laying across our little boy's bed. Luckily, he was still fast asleep. The irons and fender had been lifted by an unseen force and in one huge bundle. This may not seem such a large task until it is remembered that these fire irons and fender weighed at least a quarter of a hundredweight. The fender was solid brass, one foot tall and six feet long; the fire irons were two feet six inches long, also of solid brass and comprised of a poker, shovel and tongs. They were very heavy, so much so that I found it very hard to lift them off the bed and return them to their rightful place in front of the enormous fireplace. We lost no time in packing our things and retiring with Russell into the Friary proper, where we had slept before. We settled down at about three in the morning and never returned to the Bishop's room again!! On her return from holiday we told Mrs Twiss of our experience with a ghost. She laughed and said 'Oh yes, we have a ghost but he won't hurt you, he is a friendly one.' I thought 'Well, I don't like his playful moods, even if he is friendly!'

Chapter 47

I Move House and Take On More

Now that Mrs Twiss was widowed she was depending on me to help with the many engagements arranged in connection with the Friary. Her gardens were giving her so much pleasure in their completed state and she wanted to share that pleasure with as many people as she could, so all types of organizations were invited to her open days. I had to cycle each day from Diss and I was spending more time at the Friary than at home, so my employer decided to build me a bungalow in the grounds so I could be close to my work. This was going to be a great help to me and my wife and I lost no time in agreeing. The bungalow was completed in three months and we moved in before the winter.

Mrs Twiss was full of surprises as I was continually discovering. The next one was when she said 'Talbot, the goats will have to go. I cannot expect you to look after them with all your other duties so I am giving all of them away to my friends, except one goat, Lilac. She has been with me since I first started with goats, she is very old and would not settle anywhere else, so I want you to arrange to have her put down. It's the kindest thing to do, get that nice man from Diss who is a slaughterer to do it here and arrange it when I am away without telling me until it is all over.' I said 'Yes Madam, I will do as you say, but I don't like doing it to poor old Lilac. She knows me and will guess what I am doing.' Mrs Twiss said 'I know how you will feel, that's why I couldn't possibly be here on that day. Anyway, I know you will do your best to be kind to her.' I thought I must not put the job off for too long or I would never do it so I saw my friend Tommy who was the man to carry out the job and arranged with him to come and do it the first day my employer was away in London. That day came sooner than I expected and all went as planned and it was a great relief to me when it was over and I filled in the grave.

155

On her return, Mrs Twiss thanked me for carrying out her wishes so promptly and then sprang another one of her surprises by saying 'I have decided to keep cows!' I could not help saying 'What?' in a very surprised manner. 'Yes,' she continued, 'I have seen my friend who has some charming little Dexter cows and I said to her I must have some of these, they will make a change from goats. I will tell Talbot as soon as I get back to prepare himself for another challenge. Well Talbot, what do you think?' I was so taken aback that I remained silent for quite a long while until I was brought back to reality when Mrs Twiss said 'I will leave you to think on what I have told you and we will discuss this further as soon as I have disposed of the remaining goats to my friends.'

A few weeks after the last goat had gone, the goat stable was stripped out and converted into a cows' milking parlour with all the latest equipment for tethering the cows. All was ready for the arrival of the first of the Dexter cows of which there were two. There was also a Jersey cow to provide milk and butter to replace that provided by the goats. We were back in business and very soon found that the cows required different treatment from the goats and it was very difficult for Mrs Twiss and myself to maintain a seven-day cover on all the requirements of three cows, plus chickens, ducks and rabbits. The man who helped me in the garden did not want to get involved with the cows, so another man who lived opposite said he would help with them. This offer was accepted and the milking and caring for the cows became his responsibility.

Another surprise was soon to be unleashed, if that is the right word! It rocked me when it came! My employer again called me and said 'Talbot, I am buying a bull to go with my cows. It's only a calf as yet so I will be able to deal with it for the time being.' When the bull arrived I was full of misgivings and questioned the wisdom of such a move as we had no building strong enough to house such a creature when it got older and would pose a threat. Mrs Twiss again solved the problem by reinforcing a spare building with massive steel tubing, which, when finished, looked strong enough for the bull which anyway would only be four feet tall but needed a building such as this for safety's sake. All went well for several weeks as my employer took the new bull calf for long walks on a halter and I carried on with my work as normal. Then one day she said 'You will have to take the bull out from now on, Talbot. He is growing fast and getting much too strong for me. Besides, his horns are growing and are beginning to pose a threat to me as they are low enough to cause serious damage if he decides to butt.' I expected this to happen as I had watched the young bull getting stronger every day and had wondered how long it would be before the novelty of leading a bull round the village would wear off. So another job was added to my many daily tasks. It was not long before he began to test my strength and I was finding it hard to control him and his horns, which were straight and waist high and becoming a threat to me as he swung his head round. Something would have to be done as I was afraid if I lost control in the village he might hurt someone and he was no longer a calf people could pat on the head, he was becoming a dominant male. The vet was consulted. He soon came to the conclusion that there is only one way to control bulls. He told me that however small they are bulls can be very dangerous and can never be trusted. He advised that a ring should be put in the bull's nose and I should get a leading pole to clip into his nose so that I could lead him anywhere. The ring was duly inserted in the bull's nose, much to his disgust, and in no uncertain terms he let us know what he thought of us by charging us at the first opportunity. We had to nip smartly to one side to avoid his wrath with his now fully grown horns, but I had the answer in my hands in the shape of the lead pole which I inserted at my first chance. To my relief this brought him to a full stop much to his surprise and pain and although I did not want to hurt him at all he had to realize he must behave. It was several days before I decided to test the ring by taking him out for a short walk. He was pleased when I opened his door, he knew he was being taken out and he pawed the floor. I inserted the pole and he made a mad rush for freedom, dragging me with him. I hung on for grim death, not daring to let go in case he escaped to the village. Once outside, he went straight through a thorn hedge about four feet thick, me with him, getting scratched all over. I held on while he made a determined dash for freedom but with me hanging on to his nose with all my might, I hoped he would soon tire. This took a good five minutes before he finally succumbed, with his nose bleeding. I felt sorry for him but looking at myself I thought 'Who's feeling sorry for me?' However, this episode proved a blessing in disguise as after that day he was never any trouble and could be taken safely round the village.

The following winter Mrs Twiss went to New Zealand and as we now had a bungalow in the grounds it was thought the Friary need not be occupied. I used to put lights on at different times in rooms to make it look occupied. One Saturday night, when we had friends from Norwich staying with us for the weekend, we men had left to put the car back in the farm building after returning from a dinner dance at eleven p.m. It was a black winter's night with the wind howling and the leaves rustling and it was pouring with rain into the bargain. It was a real spooky night to be out, especially at the back of the Friary where we had to garage the car.

The Author with the Dexter bull at the Friary, Roydon.

The barn doors were closed and could only be opened with difficulty by lifting each one over the cobbled stones. My friend said to me 'It's a pity your Friary ghost doesn't come and open the garage doors for us on a night like this.' Lo and behold! The garage doors swung open without touching the cobbled stones, as easy as if there was no obstruction at all. I drove the car in and we both jumped out and ran round the building to the bungalow without stopping to shut the doors, terrified out of our lives, our feet seemingly not touching the ground. When we arrived indoors, my wife said 'You look as if you have seen a ghost, how white you both are.' My friend retorted 'Well, at least he opened the garage doors for us. I have never experienced anything like it.' He then related to the two women what had happened and finished up by saying 'No one will get me to sleep in the Friary. I don't know how you and Nora have done it all these years.' The next morning I had composed myself and went to see if the garage doors were still a bother to shut. I found I had the same difficulty as before and realized yes, there was some unseen force here somewhere. I decided not to say anything about the ghostly happenings to Mrs Twiss on her return but to let the matter rest, although my friend and I have never ceased to mention it when we meet.

To compensate my wife and I for the extra work we were now doing, Mrs Twiss used to say 'Take the car, Talbot, and you and Mrs Talbot have a day at the coast.' We were often given this treat in lieu of extra cash which suited us fine as having the use of the car meant a lot to me. We also had the use of her large house on the cliffs at Sheringham for several years for our holidays. In fact, we got so used to Sheringham that it has always been our favourite place ever since. I often turn my thoughts back to those far-off days when I first started my journey in life, always wondering what it would be like in the future. Now, here am I, married with two sons, been through a war, started out on my own since the war and had experiences of all the new inventions man has devised.

During my time at the Friary I joined the local Angling Club at Diss and it was not long before I was made secretary. This responsibility piled extra work on me and I had to attend more meetings. We then decided to form a Sea Angling Section and I had to arrange for the bait to be sent from Lowestoft every week when we were sea fishing. After a year of this, R Thorndyke who was a friend of mine, was appointed Match Secretary which considerably lightened my load. Now life seemed even better: I was doing a job I loved and was able to fish, which I also loved. However, the strain was beginning to tell. I was trying to do my job properly, looking after the animals, gardening, chauffeuring, working at the football pitch, taking part in fishing matches and spending so much time writing for both clubs and generally chasing around. I was also playing in the band weekly. Looking back, I often wonder where all my energy came from. Eventually I came to the conclusion the football job would have to go as out of the two sports, fishing came first. I could sit and relax whilst fishing, whereas the football club needed a very energetic person to run it. So, reluctantly, I resigned from the Football Club and concentrated on the Angling Club at Diss, with which I remain associated to this day. At the time of writing, however, only three of us remain from the fifty original members who were there when I first joined.

In 1956 I lost my dear mother, who had been my mainstay throughout my young life until I married at the age of twenty-eight. She had been a wonderful mother to me and I can honestly say she never once said an unkind word to me or lost her temper with me. I shall always remember her kindly look and smiling eyes. I am recording these words of thanks to her through these pages as a lasting act of respect to the one who made my life possible and so happy through the years.

At about this time of sadness, my wife lost a friend who remembered her in her will and in due course my wife received £100. She partly used the money to buy our first car, which was a 1929 Singer. It had leather straps which worked the windows like in a railway carriage and it cost £19 at a sale. It was a very reliable machine but very noisy as it had a gate change gearbox and I had to double-declutch when tackling a hill. Luckily this presented no problem to me as I had learned to use it in the petrol lorry all those years ago.

A whole new era opened up before me, I could now take my family out and about and petrol was only two shillings and sixpence (12p) a gallon and my mother-in-law always filled the petrol tank when we took her out. We enjoyed life even better than before. When visiting Sheringham for our holidays, we now had our own transport and took full advantage of that fact. As we cooked for ourselves on holiday, we would take enough potatoes and vegetables with us to last the week, quite a saving as we all enjoyed good appetites! I also found the car very useful for travelling to and from our local river to fish. It saved me getting wet when cycling and so I continued to enjoy the life now presented to me.

For the next few years, nothing seemed to alter, the seasons came and went until one day when I was returning in the car with Mrs Twiss from one of our frequent outings to some organization in which she had an interest, she sprang another one of her surprises on me. Although I was used to her sudden statements and questions, I was not prepared for what she said that day: 'When I die Talbot, what would you like to do?' I was so taken aback with these words I hardly knew how to reply. When I finally made up my mind what to say, she had lit herself another cigarette and was so composed it was unbelievable after asking such a question. 'Well Madam,' I said, 'I don't like to hear you say such things.' She insisted 'We all have to face up to these things you know and I wondered what you would like to do.' I replied 'Well Madam, as you know I help in the local pub some nights and I feel I would like to be a landlord of one.' Mrs Twiss asked 'If that's what you would like, how much would it cost you to get a pub?' When I told her what I thought it might cost, she said 'That's settled then,' and sat back to enjoy her journey home, while I was wondering all the time what had brought all this on.

A little later, on another journey home from attending a funeral of one of her close companions, she turned again to me and said 'How awful being buried. Make sure I am cremated, won't you Talbot? I don't want to be buried.' This talk about funerals and dying set me thinking again. Why was she telling me all this, did she know something, or have a premonition?

Chapter 48

Clouds Loom On The Horizon

After that last trip, I had a creepy feeling that all was not well with Mrs Twiss and to confirm my worst fears I was being asked to drive her almost everywhere, whereas before she loved driving herself about in the Vauxhall Wyvern she had just acquired. Once she snapped at something I said; quite unlike her. As the months went by it became obvious something was amiss, especially when I had to take her to a private Nursing Home for an operation which, I discovered later, was never carried out although she had us believe it had been a success. She was that sort of lady, never giving in to her pain and always making out things were as normal, which of course they were not. The next winter, instead of going abroad, she wished to spend Christmas with her sister, Lady Ethel Thomson, at her London hotel as if she knew something was going to happen to her. All the family tried to keep the news of her illness from my wife and I as they knew how devoted we were to her. This winter proved to be a very sharp one with much snow and many frosts. I kept the fires going in the Friary which heated the water but was unable to prevent the cold penetrating the house as nobody was living in it, it was always cold. Just after Christmas I had a telephone call from Mrs Twiss's daughter, Mrs Lambert, saying her mother would be coming back to the Friary on the following Thursday, bringing two nurses with her and another friend to look after everyone, cooking, etc. Mrs Twiss had said she wanted to die in her own house and so the arrangements were made with just a week to go.

I was told to get the house nice and warm and my wife was asked to prepare the beds for the two nurses and the friend, Mrs Baker, who would be in charge. We hurriedly carried out these instructions with heavy hearts. I kept the boiler going at full pelt to keep the water hot but I was not prepared for the shock to come. On the Sunday night I had fed the animals and poultry then went into the house to stoke up the boiler. As I was inserting the key in the lock I heard what I thought was a terrible downpour of rain. I thought I was imagining things. But when I opened the door, what a sight confronted me! The place was flooded with water which was pouring through the ceilings everywhere. I rushed outside to turn the stopcock off but could not move the snow quickly enough so I hurried back in and, remembering there was a stop valve in the dairy, turned that off, then rushed over to our bungalow to fetch my wife. I raked all the fire out of the boiler and threw the burning coke outside. I was then able to take stock of the damage. I remembered an old trick and fetched a walking stick and poked a few holes in the sagging ceiling to let the water out, then went upstairs to see where the burst pipe was. It was in the attic, split in several places. We then took a look in the visitor's bedroom where Mrs Baker was to sleep and found the ceiling above her bed was leaking too. The bed was soaked, what were we to do? I decided we must telephone Mrs Lambert who lived twenty miles away. When I spoke to her and explained the situation, she said 'It can't be helped. Do what you can tonight, it's a good job it's not Mother's bedroom. I will come over in the morning.' My wife pulled the wet bed linen onto the floor and propped it up against the wall, then directed the heat from the electric fire at a safe distance from it. Fortunately the bed was not soaked through as the bed clothes had absorbed most of the water and these could easily be replaced from the stock cupboard. Now to get rid of the water! This presented a mammoth task as every drop had to be mopped up by hand and squeezed into a pail, which took most of the night and half the next day. As my wife looked at the ceilings dripping water she remarked 'Sid, the Friary is crying as if it knows the worst is soon to come. Remember me saying to you last summer that all the flowers which were normally bright colours had turned mauve and purple? The garden had gone into mourning!'

Mrs Lambert came, as did Mrs Baker, who was to supervise the housekeeping. She was a great help and soon made light work of cleaning up, with my wife's assistance. I had lost heart in the garden but made sure the animals were well looked after. Mrs Twiss was brought home from London by ambulance, together with the two nurses who were to be with her night and day. I can still remember the shock I had when I first saw the shrunken body of my employer in the ambulance, and knew from that moment that the end was very near. As it happened, Mrs Twiss lived another three weeks, having constant attention from her nurses during that time, but she finally passed away on 26 January 1959. It was the saddest day of all our time at the Friary. All purpose seemed to have gone with her passing.

Mrs Lambert asked if Colonel Twiss was buried in Roydon churchyard but I told her he had been cremated and that it had been Mrs Twiss's wish to be cremated too. I told Mrs Lambert that her mother had specifically made that request to me and said I felt Mrs Twiss would not rest if she was buried. She was surprised that her mother did not want to buried at the local church to which she had been so devoted but eventually she agreed to have Mrs Twiss cremated. So it was that the last instruction I received from Mrs Twiss was followed and I had carried it out with a heavy heart.

Then came the task of disposing of the animals. Mr Bryant, who looked after the cows, received the bull which was promptly dispatched to market. The cows went to Mrs Twiss's friends and I had the job of disposing of the four cats, which had to be put down by the vet. Another job which I hated doing but one cat got away and was never seen again. Just before she died, Mrs Twiss gave her pet dog to my wife and it lived exactly a year to the day, dying in its sleep on 26 January 1960.

All the time the livestock were being dealt with, another big problem was on the horizon – what was to become of me? I was living in the bungalow in the grounds and Mrs Lambert wanted it vacant when the Friary came up for sale, sometime in April it was said. There was much coming and going by the three daughters, all trying their utmost to fix me up with another employer. I was offered several jobs which did not appeal to me as it meant getting used to another boss and I would find that hard if not impossible. Mrs Twiss could not be equalled. The husband of one of the granddaughters was a director of the Yarmouth Brewery and decided to approach me regarding the possibility of becoming a tenant of one of their pubs. Now this did appeal to me, as it was just what I wanted. My wife did not like this idea but said she would go along with me if that was what I wanted. She said she would rather have a restaurant as with a pub the house is never your own, but with the legacy Mrs Twiss left, I was able to have my first pub, which was at Stanton near Bury St Edmunds. Twelve miles away, this was quite a big decision to make. Our two sons accepted the move but were not over-excited. Anyway, we were now the Landlord and Landlady of the Stanton Cock Public House, a far cry from the peace and tranquility of the Friary!

One last job I had to perform before leaving the Friary was to go with a furniture lorry all the way to Sheringham, some 50 miles, to collect the furniture from Mrs Twiss's holiday house, and bring it back to the Friary for the forthcoming sale. This quite upset me as this visit to Sheringham reminded me of the many happy holidays we had had there, never to be repeated. One of the bitter-sweet memories of my life.

Diss and District Angling Club – Annual Dinner 1953.
L to R: The author, R Thorndyke, A Madgett, Mrs Twiss.

Chapter 49

We Knuckle Down Once More

With new zest we tackled this new challenge and found the locals of Stanton very helpful and understanding. We were accepted and welcomed as if we had been there all our lives, which was a great help to us. We soon discovered that being tenants of our own pub was not like being customers the other side of the bar! What with keeping the coal fires clean and burning, all the cellar work, and serving the long hours; then the most important work of all, the bookwork, dealing with the orders, seeing representatives, we soon found out the rigours of running a pub!

We were still young – I was 45 years old when I took the pub – and work seemed a pleasure at first. It was not long before we took in some lodgers and this added considerably to the workload but we plodded on. We were now selling more beer than was ever expected by the brewery and it was not long before the brewery carried out massive alterations to the pub and put the toilets indoors, much to everyone's delight.

We had a considerable number of bachelors in the village who spent most of their spare time in various pubs. My older son, Russell, who was also a teenager, said to me 'You know what you should do, Dad? Put some music in your large lounge bar which is hardly used, then the boys will soon come and enjoy themselves in this pub.' I asked what sort of music, and he suggested I should get a tape recorder and play some tapes. I saw one advertised and tried it out. It was an instant success but it was not long before all the tapes were torn due to the rough handling they received. One of the lads said 'Why don't you get a juke-box, Sid?' I was not sure if they were allowed in pubs but the idea appealed to me and I made enquiries at the brewery who said they had no objections if the police did not mind. They warned me to watch out that I did not attract the wrong element of custom but I felt I knew my customers enough to take a chance

165

on that happening. I enquired of a well-known juke-box firm who were only too willing to give it a trial run and it was agreed on a 50/50 basis. The great day arrived when the juke-box was installed, which caused quite a stir in the village. We even had a visit from the parson, who did not like the idea at all but he was reassured by the police, who told him it was the best move I had made. The police said 'We shall at least know where the youngsters are and they won't be getting up to mischief elsewhere.' I was very pleased at the police reaction and vowed I would do my utmost to keep a law-abiding house.

All went very well and I was soon earning as much money from the juke-box as from the pub itself. Me being me, I was soon thinking to myself 'Why should I share the takings with the juke-box company. Far better if I owned the machine and so had the lot.' I approached the company saying I would like to buy a machine and they brought me a catalogue of their latest models. I felt that if I was going to splash out on a new juke-box then I would have the latest and best one available which happened to be a Wurlitzer – the same as was fitted in the Queen Mary and Queen Elizabeth ocean-going liners. I was offered easy terms and so another great day arrived. From that day onward I never looked back, we always had a full house, much to the interest of some of my other friends and the publicans of other houses who viewed my venture with great concern. I was the first publican in West Suffolk who had the nerve to invest in such a noisy addition to the sombre nature of the pubs of the day. I knew change was coming and I had proved it, as before long most of the other pubs had installed a juke-box and found it was a welcome source of income. Mind you, I was lucky as at that time in the 1960s so many lovely songs were popular, including those by the Beatles, whose records were always in demand. Another reason for this success was the fact that I let the youngsters choose the records they wanted and I never bought any they would not approve of, so a very happy relationship developed between us.

Of course, there were many occasions when life did not always run smoothly, such as the day my wife was threatened with a beer mug by a rowdy customer. She stood and stared him out and in the end he dropped the mug to the floor and departed with his gang of roughs. They were well known at that time for their brief visits to as many pubs in one night as possible. There were up to seven of them on motor cycles and they would descend on a pub and cause as much of a disturbance as possible. They would pour beer over another customer's head and ruin his shirt and on one occasion they grabbed all the evening football papers from the customers' hands, placed them in a pile in the middle of the lounge and then set fire to them. They then grabbed more pints of beer to douse the flames. They would leave before the police arrived, and would repeat the same treatment at another pub perhaps ten miles away. The police could do nothing about it as no witness was willing to testify for fear of reprisals and the police were never able to be at the pub when all this was happening. The same gang were believed to be responsible for several incidents in the area, such as turning the signposts round so they pointed in the wrong direction. On another occasion a farmer left his combine harvester in his field of corn over the weekend and found on Monday morning that most of the machine had been dismantled and scattered over a wide area in the growing crop. One publican lost all his pint glasses by the same gang who had entered his pub, taken every glass they could find, taken them outside and smashed them against his pub wall, then departed as usual. It was on occasions like this that I wondered what had possessed me to want to lead such a life. What about my family, particularly my younger son, Raymond? Putting the question to them on many occasions, I always received the same answer – 'You wanted to do this and we will have to put up with it and make the best of it,' and so we carried on.

It was an interesting public house as it was also the doctor's surgery for the village. Two days a week the doctor would be in attendance from Hopton, a village some four miles away. Medicine and tablets were left later in the day for the patients to collect. On Sunday, the lounge would be used as a Roman Catholic church as we had Americans in the area who were devout Roman Catholics. The ladies' toilet area would be used as a confessional! Their service was always early in the morning so as not to interfere with the opening of the pub.

I had an antique brass bell which was kept on the counter for customers to ring when they required service. One day, it was missing after some servicemen had left the pub. I did not want to prosecute but I wanted it back, so I wrote to the Commanding Officer at the local RAF station, saying I believed one of their personnel had taken it and if it was returned no more would be said. Imagine my surprise the next day when a service vehicle pulled up outside the pub. Out jumped two RAF Police officers, escorting an individual airman, together with another high-ranking officer, who formed up outside the pub. Then, with shouts and orders and much clicking of heels, they entered the bar and all stood to attention facing me. The officer ordered 'Step forward and return the item'. The poor man coloured up, took two paces forward and said to me 'I am sorry for taking your property, here is your bell. I will never do this again.' I did not know how to reply, all I could think of was 'That's all right, I am sure you won't.' With more clicking of heels and words of command, the party left. I don't know who felt the more sick, me or that young man. I felt guilty at reporting the loss, somehow the bell did not seem important any more. This was especially so as I heard through the grapevine that the airman had been very severely dealt with back at the camp. We had a great many happy incidents as well. One customer looked on me as his doctor, as when he had indulged the night before, I always left a bottle of my strongest ale under a shrub near the front door of the pub last thing before going to bed. This would be retrieved by my hung-over friend on his way to work at 5.30 a.m. It was, I was assured, a certain cure for whatever ailment he was suffering from. He swore by it and always called me Dr Talbot.

One day the local council roadman came to the back door pushing his wheelbarrow which contained about twenty small bottles of beer. He said 'I believe these are yours, Sid,' and I asked how it was that he had them. He told me he had found them in the ditch at the bottom of the street and said 'I reckon chaps from the camp pinched them and got the wind up while they were waiting for a taxi to take them back to the camp so they dumped them.' I wondered how they had got them without me seeing but I very soon found out. On looking around I discovered several bottles were missing from a display quite near a sash window which could easily be opened. All they had to do was reach in and grab the bottles one by one and pass them to an accomplice. I did nothing about it as this was my fault for putting temptation within easy reach.

I learned several lessons whilst a Landlord. Especially not to trust everyone, as I had one regrettable experience while doing that once too often. We had a few lodgers and my wife warned me about trusting one of them. I did not heed her warning as I trusted everyone, until the local grocer remarked 'Do you know if one of your lodgers gets paid in half-crowns as he always pays in silver when buying cigarettes from my shop? I would be a bit worried if I were you, as you can't lock your bar up and you have an open till and always keep lots of change. I would check up if I were you.'

'I told you so,' said my wife. 'That's where our money is going,' but I said we could not prove anything and would have to catch him in the act. Our pub was so designed that we had to go through the bars to get to the ladies' toilet, the only inside toilet at that time which, as occupants of the house, we used during the night. One Saturday we were having our lunch when this suspect disappeared to the toilet. After a long time had elapsed,

my wife said 'He's up to something, creep up to the bar and have a look.'
I did and what I saw confirmed my wife's worst suspicions, there was our
lodger helping himself to silver from our till and stuffing it in his pocket. I
just stood there staring until he turned round and saw me. He replaced the
money and with a bluster about wanting some change he did a frantic exit
from the bar to his bedroom. When I returned to my lunch, my wife said
'What did I tell you? I knew he was no good all along. He will have to go,
it's not fair on our other nice lodgers being under the same roof as a thief.'
With a triumphant look on her face indicating she had been proved right,
she cleared the table leaving me to ponder on the method I would use to
get rid of him. As it happened, it was achieved in a way I had not thought
possible as, when our three honest and respectable lodgers heard about it,
they said 'Leave him to us, we never liked him anyway.' That night they
told him to pack his bags which he did as although he was a big man he
was a coward at heart. He was bundled into their Land Rover and driven
ten miles to Bury St Edmunds where they bundled him out, together with
his luggage and they left him with the words 'That's for treating Nora and
Sid the way you did. Don't come back!' We never saw him again and I
learned my lesson once again not to trust everyone at first sight.

After we got used to running the Cock, life seemed to have taken on a
new meaning for us, we had a new army of friends, especially as the
Football Club had made its headquarters at the pub.

However, after six years, the trade was at its maximum and the strain
was beginning to tell. It was becoming a burden to us and no longer the
pleasure it had been. I was the first to pay the penalty of working so hard,
suffering a heart problem, and I was warned by the hospital to either give
up the pub life or take a smaller one. For a whole year prior to this my
wife had more or less borne the responsibility of running the pub which
was no mean task. A pub can be a very tiring place and when all the
customers had gone and we were left with an empty pub a feeling of
loneliness stole over us, a feeling hard to explain. At that time the pub
where I played bowls in Diss came up for letting and as I had been warned
about my health I asked the brewery if I could transfer to this smaller pub.
They agreed, and so we made the move back to Diss and became the
Landlord and Landlady of 'The Cherry Tree'. My family did not like the
idea at all but as I pointed out I could no longer continue working the
other pub, once more I had my own way.

Chapter 50

Out of The Frying Pan . . .

My wife warned me 'Are you sure we have done right by coming here? I have a feeling you will regret it. I feel we should have stuck it out and paid someone to do your work at the Cock. Still, we are here now and will have to make the most of it.'

It was not long before my wife was again proved right as, within a few weeks trading, we found that instead of making things better for ourselves, we were much worse off. The takings were so much in contrast to what we had been used to, it was frightening. We did not take as much in a week at the Cherry Tree as we took in a lunchtime at the Cock. We had a fair amount of trade from the Bowls Club in the summer but in the winter very few wanted to know and we had to rely on a very small number of faithful customers to keep us going. It was such a bleak outlook that my wife was forced to return to her old job of catering in the town to augment our meagre income. We could not use our juke-box which we had taken with us as one of the locals threatened 'If you use that thing we will leave you. We don't want that sort of row going on in here. I will warn you now, this is a quiet pub, how we like it.' So I was forced to knuckle down to their wishes. It was not long before I began to resent this sort of life but I did my best to improve trade. I floodlit the bowling green to extend the season but although the idea was all right in theory, in practice I had not allowed for the cold weather so after a few matches we had to abandon this idea. By this time I was getting really fed up, particularly when my wife reminded me of her former misgivings with 'I told you so'. In the end I said 'I am going to pack it in, if I can find myself a job. But who wants anybody at my age?' I was then 52 years old and the hope of being employed again was very remote.

However, at that time Etheridges Stores back in Stanton were having a bit of bother with their manager and were looking for a reliable replacement. My son's young lady, Heather, worked in the store and, knowing how much I wanted to quit the pub trade, spoke up for me to the owners of the store, Ridleys of Bury St Edmunds. I went for an interview, not expecting to be selected due to my background of pub life, but after a small intelligence test I was told I could have the job which included a house and £12 10 shillings a week pay.

On accepting this job I had to promise my wife and two sons I would not subject them to any more moves. This would have to be my final one until I reached retirement age. I readily accepted this condition as I was prepared to try anything to be free of life at the pub. I felt it was a chance we must take. I think they were pleased to return to Stanton as many friends had been made during the six years at the pub and we would not be moving amongst strangers this time.

Chapter 51

Jack of All Trades

We duly moved back to Stanton and prepared for another new challenge. Our boys had both found jobs in an engineering firm in the village so for a time anyway we were all settled.

The first day or two at the shop my wife and I were getting to know the staff and where everything was kept. This was quite different from the trade we had been used to, as it was well and truly one of the old-fashioned stores which sold everything from tin tacks to knicker elastic! We had a complete ladies' department, with a lovely brass measure screwed to the mahogany counter for elastic, ribbon, lace and curtain material to be measured. We sold ironmongery of all descriptions – nails by the hundredweight for which we had to climb upstairs. Also upstairs were the boots and shoes. Rubber boots hung all round the ceiling beams in the shop, as did pots and pans, kettles etc., and chopping hooks for firewood. Then there were the oil lamps and lanterns. Outside were the massive paraffin tanks from which several hundred gallons were sold each week. Inside was that lethal weapon, the bacon slicer, which claimed someone's fingers every week when being cleaned. A very dangerous machine to use, but efficient. We had whole sides of bacon delivered to us, Heather was the expert in boning, although we all had to learn each other's jobs. We were agents for a dry cleaning firm and for the Eastern Counties Bus Company, booking people's tickets for long distance journeys. We were also collecting agents for parcels. On top of all these many duties, we had a considerable paper round, which many children did before attending school. To prevent the firm from getting into trouble over the employment of children, I told the youngsters that if they wanted to carry on with their paper rounds they would have to come to an agreement with each of the households they were taking the papers to. They had to

The author and Marion Mulley, one of the shop assistants, outside Etheridge's Stores, Stanton.

ask the person concerned to pay what the boy or girl wanted. This idea worked well because officially we were then employing no one for deliveries and the children were more than satisfied as they could charge more than they had been getting before. The people could either pay their price or fetch the papers themselves! Of course the main purpose of the store was the comprehensive stock of groceries. We even had a small delivery van in which we still delivered to some of the older customers in the country who had been dealing with the shop for years and who were reluctant to change their ways by going to the few supermarkets which were beginning to spring up.

Here was I, now in charge of what was a valuable outlet to my employers, a job I had never ever been trained for and a far cry from the distant past when I watched the women stone-picking. I had some doubts as to whether I would be able to learn all there was to know about so many things. At the same time, keeping the books correctly was the most important task to worry about, a job I felt I had a flair for but for which I had had no previous training. I was able to master the job with the excellent help of the staff and the patience of Ridleys, who let me gradually assume control in my own time. One of their directors came every week to help with the books and the wages until I felt able to cope alone.

In 1971 the new method of counting our money and consequently some new coins, were introduced and to get us used to these I decided to have all the staff in on the Sunday prior to the changeover. We each took a basket (we had become a self-service store by then) and filled it up and took it in turns to go to the checkout until we were all confident of what we were doing and felt familiar with the new system. So, when the first customers arrived on the Monday morning, we were all prepared and made few mistakes, although most of the customers were very confused and it took some of them months to get used to the new money.

At last we were feeling happy about life and things progressed at a steady pace. We thought this job would see us through to retirement age but we had no idea what was around the corner to change our way of life yet again.

Chapter 52

More Changes

The first news we had that changes were on the way was when we were told a new young director had taken over the firm and he was full of ideas to update the business. The first alteration was the building of a warehouse on a disused aerodrome to be used as a 'cash and carry' store. This was quickly followed by the selling of all Ridley's outlying shops which eventually meant ours. This came as a great blow to us. Here we were, just nicely established, when we were given three months notice to quit the premises as a buyer had been found. I admit we were given first refusal but we could not raise the cash for such a venture and so once more we had to look for somewhere to live. Everyone in the village felt very sorry for us, including the policeman, who went out of his way to try to help us find a place to go. Things were getting desperate for us as the buyers from London wanted possession. As a temporary measure a caravan was installed in the yard of the shop so the new owner could live there while I taught her the business. At the same time Ridleys had rented a cottage for me further up the street. I taught the new owner all I could in the short time I had left and even she felt sorry for us but there was nothing that could be done to ease the pressure we found ourselves in, it had all happened so quickly.

The weeks seemed to fly with us getting no further in our search for a home. I was 59 years old and it was a certainty I would never find a place of employment at that age. While on a visit to Diss one day we noticed a bungalow in Roydon for sale for £4,750. A bit pricey at that time but it was a very good property. It was just what we wanted, so after another family conference we decided to have a go. I approached the building society who said as my son Raymond lived with me and he was at work I could get a mortgage, provided his name was included in the deeds. We hastily filled forms and moved in almost at once. We had made a good move here, but how was I going to repay the mortgage? I told my wife 'I am going to buy the lease on the greengrocer's shop in Diss and earn a living from there.' My wife responded with 'I am going back to my old job in catering in Diss – you please yourself what you do.' I had a feeling she was just getting a bit fed up with me and my moves but, as I pointed out, all the moves had been forced on me. Anyway, I had worked for Mrs Twiss for fifteen years and had she not died I would have still been there. I had such wonderful memories of my time working at the Friary and on the day she died walking in the house was like walking in a cathedral – a very celestial feeling, so hard to explain. I remember thinking at the time 'It's the passing of a saint' – such was my respect for her.

So, I bought the lease of the shop in Diss and started trading at once. I was used to selling greengrocery as we sold quite a lot at Stanton. The trade was quite good and I was happy enough there until one day a lady came into the shop and said to me 'It's a pity you don't bring some of these nice fruit and vegetables home with you and sell to us from your bungalow at Roydon. It is opposite where they are building a new estate and we are the first of several hundred who will eventually be living there.' I thought a lot about what she had said and for a trial period I took orders at Roydon and sold the goods from my bungalow. This was such a success I decided to sell the shop in Diss and concentrate on Roydon. All went very well for a long time, the housing estate filled up and trade became good selling from my garage until someone reported me to the Council and I was told to stop trading. However, the whole village signed a petition for me to stay, I had the backing of the local council, and support from the political party which was in power at the time who had their local headquarters in Diss. The local papers were full of the story and eventually the council relented and gave me a licence to continue to trade there. I traded from my garage at Roydon until well past my 65th birthday and this proved to be my best move ever.

Chapter 53

Heartbreak as I Enter The Final Straight

I am now presumably nearing the end of my life's journey of happiness and tears and yes, I have experienced both those emotions many times during my long life. Every time a friend or acquaintance passed on a great feeling of loss always left me feeling sad, but I have been happy to have known them at some stage of my life. My greatest loss was when I was 75 years old and we lost our older son, Russell, at the age of 45. We feel thankful as both sons have blessed us with grandchildren – seven between them, and we now have two great-grandchildren. Of course, we also have two daughters-in-law to compensate us as we journey on.

There are many stories left untold in recording my memories through these chapters, to tell them all would be asking me to write another volume, which I feel would be too much for me. The stories I have told here have come from my heart, an experience I never thought would happen to me. I have heard all sorts of sayings in my time and this one from the older generation I think illustrates the true meaning of life:

<u>The Clock of Life</u>
The clock of life is wound but once
And no one has the power
To tell just when the hands will stop
At late or early hour.
Now is the only time you own;
Live, love, toil with a will,
Place no faith in tomorrow
For the clock may then be still.

I think this sums up all we need to know.

As I am now well past my 'Sell-by date' and have lived my life over again through these chapters, I feel I have enjoyed 'Two bites of the cherry'. Alas, my memories must remain as that straw in the hedge, plucked from a harvest wagon long gone!

Glossary of Special Events

In 1941 my wife and I married at St Mary's Church in Diss and enjoyed the presence of the Diss Fire Brigade who formed a Guard of Honour. We also received the very last greetings telegram to be sent out from Diss Post Office, wishing us every success from the Diss Fire Brigade. This I have still, and will always treasure. This practice of sending greetings telegrams was never again used, a great pity I think.

My wife has coped well with the life we shared together and we had two wonderful sons, Russell and Raymond. When our first son, Russell, was born and I visited them in the Nursing Home I promptly fainted. So much for my tough guy image! Raymond was born seven years later in our house and I must have improved by then as I watched the complete birth with no after-effects. A truly wonderful experience.

Russell is no longer with us but he left a wife, Heather, and four lovely children and two grandchildren of his own – our great-grandchildren. Raymond is married to Jacqueline, who mothered three wonderful sons.

Yes, I can look back on my long life and say I have been blessed.

In 1920 the humble potato crisp was invented, complete with its little bag of salt. It came on the market two years later in 1922. Insignificant? Perhaps, but it has become part of every day life and so must rate as a special event – just a thought!

The Author's wedding to Nora, 1941.

My sons – Raymond on the left, Russell on the right.